The Subcontinent of India

Regional Studies Series

The Regional Studies Series

Africa
China
Europe
The Subcontinent of India
Japan and Korea
Latin America
The Middle East and North Africa
Russia and the Commonwealth

The Subcontinent of India

Regional Studies Series

Consultants

Donald Johnson

Jean Johnson

GLOBE BOOK COMPANY
A Division of Simon & Schuster
Paramus, New Jersey

Milton Jay Belasco

Milton Jay Belasco is former Chairman of the Department of Social Studies at the William Howard Taft High School in New York City.

Harold E. Hammond

Harold E. Hammond is Professor Emeritus of History in the College of Arts and Sciences at New York University.

Area specialists: Donald Johnson is Director of the Asian Studies Program in the College of Arts and Sciences of New York University and Professor of International Education in NYU,s College of Education. Jean Johnson is a teacher of Asian Studies at the Friends Seminary in New York City.

Executive Editor: Stephen Lewin
Project Editor: Samuel C. Plummer
Art Director: Nancy Sharkey
Cover Designer: Armando Baez
Production Manager: Winston Sukhnanand
Marketing Manager: Elmer Ildefonso

Cover Image: The picture on the cover shows a marketplace in Udaipur, Rajasthan, India.
Maps: Mapping Specialists, Ltd.
Graphs, Diagrams, and Charts: Keithley and Associates

Photographic acknowledgments appear on page 212.

ISBN 835-90423-7

CONTENTS

Maps

Graphs, Charts, and Diagrams

India is a country with a tremendous vitality, which it has shown throughout its history. It has often enough imposed its own cultural pattern on other countries not by force of arms, but by the strength of her vitality, culture, and civilization. There is no reason why we should give up our way of doing things. . . . We should approach [our] problems, whether domestic or international problems, in our own way.

—Jawaharlal Nehru

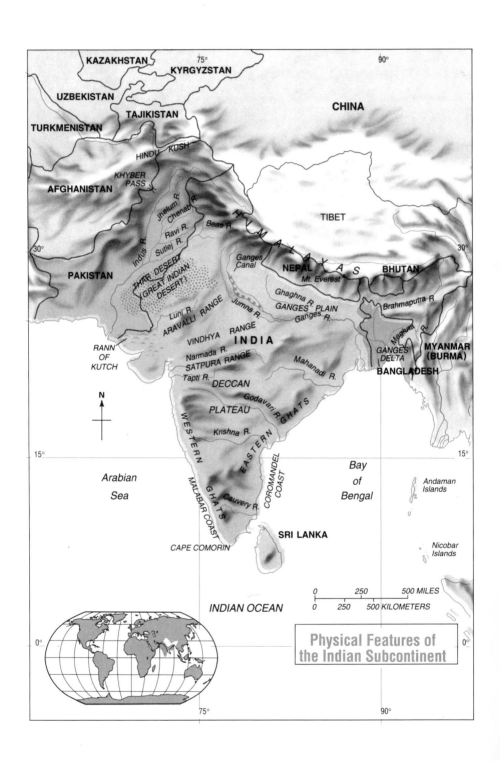

KAZAKHSTAN   75°   90°
    KYRGYZSTAN

UZBEKISTAN
                              CHINA
        TAJIKISTAN
TURKMENISTAN

        HINDU KUSH

    KHYBER
AFGHANISTAN PASS

                Jhelum R.
            Chenab R.
        Ravi R. Beas R.   TIBET
    Indus R.
30°   Sutlej R.   30°

PAKISTAN   THAR DESERT   Ganges
        (GREAT INDIAN   Canal   NEPAL   BHUTAN
        DESERT)   Mt. Everest

                    Ghaghna R.   Brahmaputra R.
            Luni R.   RANGE Jumna R. GANGES PLAIN
        ARAVALLI   Ganges R.
                VINDHYA RANGE
RANN   I N D I A   GANGES   MYANMAR
OF   Narmada R.   DELTA   (BURMA)
KUTCH   SATPURA RANGE   Mahanadi R. BANGLADESH

        Tapti R.
            DECCAN
N   Godavari R.
↑   PLATEAU
                    Krishna R.

15°   15°

Arabian   Andaman
                                Islands
Sea   MALABAR COAST Cauvery R. COROMANDEL COAST Bay
                                of
                            Bengal   Nicobar
                                    Islands
        CAPE COMORIN   SRI LANKA

                            0   250   500 MILES
            INDIAN OCEAN   0   250   500 KILOMETERS

0°   Physical Features of   0°
                        the Indian Subcontinent

            75°   90°

1 The Indian Subcontinent: Land and Peoples

The subcontinent of India is in South Asia. It is called a **subcontinent** because of its huge size and because its topographical features set it off from the rest of Asia. The subcontinent is divided among three nations: India, Pakistan (pak-ih-STAN), and Bangladesh (bahng-gluh-DESH).

THE LAND

The subcontinent of India is shaped like a huge triangle. The broad northern top of the triangle is separated from much of the rest of Asia by the towering, snow-covered Himalayas (him-uh-LAY-uhz), the tallest mountains in the world. *Himalaya* means "home of snow." The point of the triangle juts into the Indian Ocean on the south. In the north, its neighbors are the People's Republic of China; Tibet (tih-BET), which is controlled by China; and the two small countries of Nepal (nuh-PAWL) and Bhutan (boo-TAN). In the east, India has a long border with Myanmar, formerly known as Burma. India also shares a long border with Bangladesh, which it almost completely surrounds. On the west, Pakistan and India share a border from the coast north to Kashmir (KASH-mihr). Pakistan, in turn, has a long border on the north and west with Afghanistan and a somewhat shorter border with Iran to the west. The tip of the triangle, Cape Comorin (KAHM-uh-run), with the Arabian Sea on the west, and the Bay of Bengal (ben-GAWL) on the east, is separated by about 70 miles (112 km) from the island nation of Sri Lanka (sree-LAHNG-kuh), formerly known as Ceylon (suh-LAHN).

The area of the Indian subcontinent is about 1,633,000 square miles (4,230,000 square km), or less than half the size of the United States. There are about 1.1 *billion* people in the subcontinent, more than four times the number in the United States. India accounts for more than three-fourths of the subcontinent in both area and population, with about 1,270,000 square miles (3,290,000 square km) and a population of about 844 million. Its area, about one-third the size of the United States, makes India the seventh largest country in the world. India's population is the second largest in the world. Only China has more people.

Pakistan, with an area of about 310,000 square miles (800,000 square km), is slightly larger than the combined size of Texas and Louisiana. Bangladesh, at about 56,000 square miles (145,000 square km), is about the size of Illinois. Despite their relatively small sizes, both countries have large populations. Their populations of 118 million (Bangladesh) and 113 million (Pakistan) make them the seventh and eighth most populous nations on earth. Together, the populations of the three nations of the subcontinent almost equal China's.

It is important to note that before 1947 the entire subcontinent was united under one government. From 1947 to 1971, there were two nations on the subcontinent, India and Pakistan, both part of India until the partition in 1947. Pakistan's two parts were separated by nearly 1,000 miles (1,600 km), with India between them. In 1971 the eastern part of Pakistan became the independent nation of Bangladesh, while the western part continued as Pakistan.

Geographic Areas of India.   The lofty Himalayas on the northern border of India and the Hindu Kush mountains of Pakistan slope into hills that descend into the great Lowland plain. The plain spreads from east to west across the broad part of the triangle, including most of Bangladesh and much of Pakistan. In the south it extends to the Vindhya (VIN-dyuh) Mountains, which separate it from the great Deccan (DEK-uhn) plateau to the south. The Deccan, in turn, is separated from the sea by mountain ranges called the Eastern Ghats (GAHTS) and Western Ghats, which run parallel to the eastern and western coasts. Between these mountain ranges and the coasts there are coastal plains. Thus, the subcontinent of India is divided into four major geographical areas:

- The Himalayas
- The Lowland plain
- The Deccan plateau
- The Southern coastal plains

The Himalayas.   The most impressive geographic feature of India is the great Himalaya mountain range. It stretches across the top of India

A goatherd tends his small flock in a valley of the Himalayas. The rugged mountains in the background are typical of the entire Himalayas range.

in a curve that is more than 1,500 miles (3,600 km) long and 150 to 200 miles (240 to 320 km) wide. Its western extension, the Hindu Kush, curves through Pakistan and Afghanistan almost to the Arabian Sea. The mountain ranges form a natural boundary for India.

The mountains create a wall that averages over 17,000 feet (5,180 meters) high. There are many mountain peaks that rise to 25,000 feet (7,620 meters). The tallest, Mt. Everest at the Nepal–Tibet border, at 29,028 feet (8,848 meters) is the highest point on earth.

The mountains are important for several reasons:

- Travel across the mountains is difficult. There are no railroads, and even flying across the mountains is dangerous. There are, however, a few passes in the western part of the mountain range through which foreign peoples have invaded India. The most famous of these is the Khyber (KEYE-buhr) Pass through the Hindu Kush between Afghanistan and Pakistan.

- The mountains block the cold winds that blow southward out of Tibet and central Asia, and thus protect northern India from frost and freezing cold.

3

CASE STUDY:
The Vale of Kashmir

The Vale (valley) of Kashmir, in the north, is one of the most scenic parts of the Indian subcontinent. V. S. Naipaul describes his arrival there with a busload of Indian tourists. Naipaul is a native of Trinidad, in the West Indies, where his grandparents had immigrated from India.

> It was night, clear and cold, when we stopped at Banihal. . . . In the moonlight the terraced rice fields were like leaded panes of glass. In the morning their character had changed. They were green and muddy. After the Banihal tunnel we began to go down and down, past fairytale villages set in willow groves, watered by rivulets with grassy banks, into the Vale of Kashmir.
>
> Kashmir was coolness and colour: the yellow mustard fields, the mountains, snow-capped, the milky blue sky in which we rediscovered the drama of clouds. It was men wrapped in brown blankets against the morning mist, and barefooted shepherd boys with caps and covered ears on steep wet rocky slopes. . . .
>
> The mountains receded. The valley widened into soft, well-watered fields. The road was lined with poplars and willows drooped on the banks of clear rivulets. Abruptly, at Awantipur, out of a fairytale village of sagging wood-framed cottages there rose ruins of grey stone, whose heavy trabeate* construction—solid square pillars on a portico [porch], steep stone pediments [gables] on a colonnade [row of columns] around a central shrine, massive and clumsy in ruin— caused the mind to go back centuries to ancient worship. They were Hindu ruins, of the eighth century, as we discovered later. But none of the passengers exclaimed, none pointed. They lived among ruins; the Indian earth was rich with ancient sculpture.

---

* trabeate, built with horizontal beams or with lintels (horizontal stones resting on pillars), rather than with arches

V. S. Naipaul, *An Area of Darkness*. New York: Macmillan, 1964, pp. 101–102.

1. Does the Vale of Kashmir sound, from this description, like a place you would like to visit? Explain.

2. How does Naipaul's attitude toward the ruins differ from that of his fellow passengers? How does Naipaul explain this difference?

- The Indian subcontinent's main rivers have their sources in the Himalayas. The Ganges (GAN-jeez), the Jumna (JUM-nuh), the Indus, the Brahmaputra (brahm-uh-POO-truh), and their branches, all rise in these mountains. They receive a steady supply of water from the melting snows and glaciers of the Himalayas. They do not depend for their water on rainfall, which in most parts of India occurs only a few months each year. Their year-round water supply is vital to the hundreds of millions of people who live in the northern plains that are watered by these rivers.

- The Himalayan wall has an important effect on the Indian monsoon (mahn-SOON) winds, which blow northeastward from the Indian Ocean until they hit the mountains. The winds rise and cool, and the water vapor forms rain that falls on the Lowland plains. (The importance of the monsoons on Indian life will be examined later in this chapter.)

The mountains taper down in the east to the steaming jungle of Assam (uh-SAM) and to the burning Thar (TAHR) Desert in the west. Thus, the mountains, the desert, and the jungle, sprawling across the top of the Indian triangle from west to east, cut the Indian subcontinent off from much of the rest of Asia.

The Lowland Plain. The mountains slope gradually into the Lowland plain, which stretches for 2,000 miles (3,200 km) from northern Pakistan across India and into Bangladesh. This flat, fertile land is watered by the

A terraced hillside in northern India. Terraces, or platforms of earth built into a hillside, make it possible to irrigate hilly land.

great rivers of India—the Ganges, the Brahmaputra, the Indus, and their tributaries. The plain is about 200 miles (320 km) wide and forms one of the largest areas of farmland in the world. It is known as "the breadbasket of India."

The continual deposits of **alluvium**, or rich topsoil, brought down from the mountains by the rivers make the plain fertile. Rainfall here averages from 40 to 80 inches (100 to 200 cm.) a year.

Nearly two-thirds of the subcontinent's people live in this area. Here are found more villages, more irrigated, productive land, and more industry than anywhere else in these countries. Half of the subcontinent's big cities are located here.

The Deccan Plateau. The Vindhya Range is the southern limit of this great plain. These mountains separate the Lowland plain from the Indian peninsula to the south. The peninsula is entirely in India. Most of it is taken up by a large plateau known as the Deccan. This broad, flat tableland is from 1,000 to 3,000 feet (915 meters) above sea level.

The Deccan is cut off from the Arabian Sea on the west and the Bay of Bengal on the east by two rugged mountain ranges, the Western and Eastern Ghats, which run parallel to the coasts. *Ghat* means "high or elevated place." The Western Ghats, with 7,000-foot (2,135-meter) peaks, rise abruptly about 30 miles (48 km) inland from the seacoast. They are difficult to climb, and there are only a few passes in their 800-mile (1,300-km) length. The Eastern Ghats are lower. The mountains average about 2,000 feet (610 meters) high.

The Ghats are high enough to prevent the summer monsoons from bringing adequate rain to much of the Deccan plateau. Rain, falling generally during the summer months, varies from 20 to 40 inches (50 to 100 cm.) per year. Alluvial deposits are not left by the rivers that flow through this region. In fact, many of these rivers dry up during periods of drought. Much of India's mineral wealth is found in the Deccan plateau.

The Southern Coastal Plains. Fertile, alluvial plains stretch along both coasts of the peninsula between the Ghats and the sea. In these long coastal plains, rainfall varies between 80 and 200 inches (200 to 500 cm.) a year. Population density is high in these areas of heavy rains, warm climate, and fertile soil. More people per square mile live along the western, or Malabar (MAL-uh-bahr), coast than in any part of the Ganges valley.

6

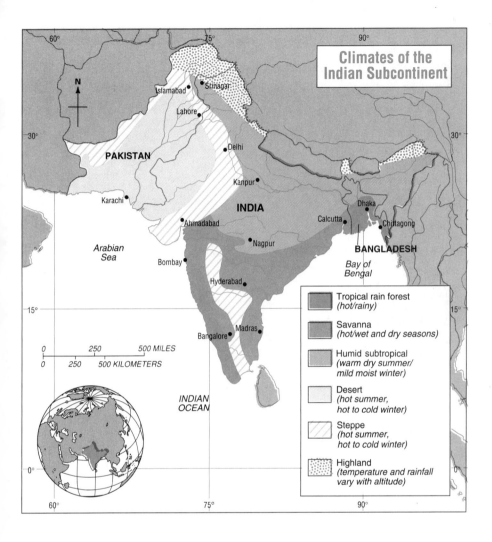

Climates of the
Indian Subcontinent

PAKISTAN

INDIA

BANGLADESH

Arabian
Sea

Bay of
Bengal

INDIAN
OCEAN

Islamabad • Srinagar
Lahore •
Delhi •
Kanpur •
Karachi •
Ahmadabad •
Nagpur •
Bombay •
Hyderabad •
Dhaka •
Calcutta • Chittagong
Bangalore • Madras •

0   250   500 MILES
0   250   500 KILOMETERS

60°   75°   90°
30°   30°
15°   15°
0°   0°

N

Tropical rain forest
(hot/rainy)

Savanna
(hot/wet and dry seasons)

Humid subtropical
(warm dry summer/
mild moist winter)

Desert
(hot summer,
hot to cold winter)

Steppe
(hot summer,
hot to cold winter)

Highland
(temperature and rainfall
vary with altitude)

CLIMATE

Within the vast area of the subcontinent, climate varies from the bitter cold of the Himalayas to the hot, steaming humidity of the jungles. The parched dryness of the western Thar Desert contrasts with the soggy wetness of eastern Assam. The climate the people experience depends upon where in the subcontinent they live.

In Bangladesh and in much of India, there are only three seasons each year: the hot and rainy season, the cool season, and the dry season. When it is hot, it is *very* hot. When it is cold, it can be uncomfortable if there is no heat in the houses. In the dry season, often no rain will fall

7

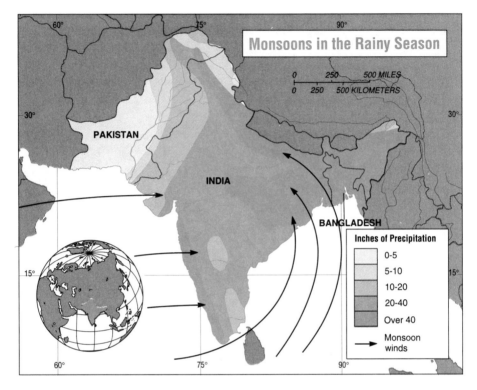

Monsoons in the Rainy Season

Inches of Precipitation
- 0-5
- 5-10
- 10-20
- 20-40
- Over 40

→ Monsoon winds

for weeks at a time. In the wet season, there often are heavy showers several times a day.

In the northern hills, temperatures sometimes fall below 0°F (–18°C), while in the Ganges lowland and the Deccan plateau, temperatures often reach 120°F (49°C). From December to March, the temperature on the coastal plains, washed by the warm waters of the Bay of Bengal and the Arabian Sea, is always between 70°F and 90°F (21°C to 32°C). It is dry in most of the country, with warm days and cool nights.

The warm season begins in April. The hottest month is May. Dry weather continues, temperatures are high, and dust storms are frequent. In the coastal areas the humidity is great because the air is heavy with the moisture that is being picked up from the nearby waters.

The rainy season follows the hot weather from June to September. Humidity is high, temperatures are a bit lower, and mildew is a constant problem.

The most comfortable months are October and November, after the rainy season is over. The sun shines, the temperatures rise, and the air is less humid.

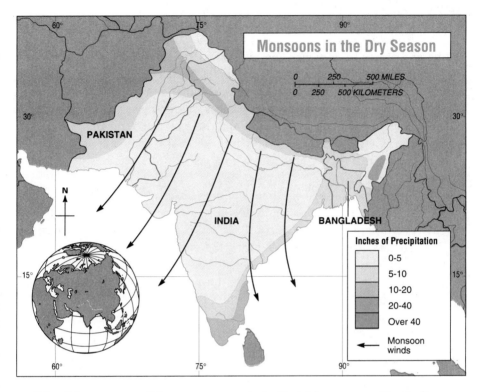

The Monsoons. Monsoons are winds that blow across the Indian Ocean and the lands near it, including the Indian subcontinent. The so-called summer monsoon blows from the southwest across the land, bringing heavy rains from June to September. The winter monsoon, which blows in the opposite direction, is cool and dry.

In most of the subcontinent, the very life of the people depends upon the summer monsoon. More than 80 percent of the annual rainfall is brought by the monsoons. If the monsoon winds do not arrive on time or do not bring sufficient rain, the land dries up and the food crop is poor. In the past, such conditions brought the threat of famine and death to many people. In other years, too much rain may bring floods that take thousands of lives. When the rains come on time, however, and in the right quantity, the fields are green, crops grow, and there is more than enough food to feed the hundreds of millions of people.

During the months of March, April, and May, the sun heats the Indian subcontinent. The air above the land gets warm, and it rises like steam from a big oven. This low pressure area draws in warm, moist air from the Indian Ocean. From June to September the summer monsoon blows this moisture-laden air in a northeasterly direction over much of

9

India. As the wind hits the Western Ghats, it begins to drop its moisture. Rain falls in great quantities along the coastal plains and western slopes of these mountains. The mountains, however, keep the Deccan plateau from getting more than a moderate rainfall.

The winds continue north of the Deccan and drop their rain south of the Himalayan Mountains. The Ganges valley receives nine-tenths of its annual 40-inch (100-cm.) rainfall in a three-month period. New York City also receives 40 inches of rain annually, but it receives two to four inches a month throughout the whole year—not 36 inches in three months.

Some places in India and Bangladesh get over 80 inches (200 cm.) of rain. In Cherrapunji (chair-uh-POON-jee), a village in Assam in northeastern India, the average rainfall is 450 inches (1,125 cm.) a year! Raindrops as big as marbles fall during the monsoon season, and the villagers must protect themselves against their sting. On the other hand, Pakistan, western India, and northwestern India are almost missed by the monsoon. They get eight or less inches (20 cm.) of rain a year.

The coming of the summer monsoon is eagerly awaited by the people. One Indian author* described its arrival in the following way:

> . . . There is a flash of lightning . . . the wind fills the black sails of the
> clouds. . . . A profound shadow falls on the earth. There is another
> clap of thunder. Big drops of rain fall and dry up in the dust. A
> fragrant smell rises from the earth. Another flash of lightning and
> another crack of thunder like the roar of a hungry tiger. It has come!
> Sheets of water, wave after wave. . . . All work stops. . . .
> Once it is on, it stays for two months or more. . . . The earth
> becomes a big stretch of swamp and mud. Wells and lakes fill up and
> burst their bounds. In towns, gutters get clogged and streets become
> turbid streams. In villages, mud walls of huts melt in the water and
> thatched [straw] roofs sag and descend on the inmates. . . . Rivers . . .
> suddenly turn to floods. . . . Roads, railway tracks and bridges go
> under water. Houses near the riverbanks are swept down to the sea.
> With the monsoon, the tempo of life and death increases. Almost
> overnight grass begins to grow and leafless trees turn green. . . .
> Snakes, centipedes and scorpions are born out of nothing. . . . Inside
> rooms the hum of mosquitoes is maddening. While the monsoon
> lasts, the showers start and stop without warning. . . . Lightning and
> thunder never cease."

---

* From *Majra*, by Khushwant Singh.

During the monsoon, the danger of floods is great. Without the monsoon, however, there is no rain at all, or in such small amounts as to create serious food problems.

Since ancient times, dams, canals, and reservoirs have been built to store the water when there is too much, so it can be released when there is not enough rain. Because of these irrigation systems, India has more irrigated land than any other country in the world.

RIVERS

The Indian subcontinent has three major river systems: The Indus and its tributaries in the west, the Ganges and its tributaries in the central and eastern part, and the Brahmaputra system in Assam in the east. Between peninsular India and the Himalayas lie the alluvial plains enriched by these three great rivers. They rise in the mountains and water the most productive and densely populated section of the subcontinent.

The Indus. The Indus River has been so important in the history of India that the Greeks gave its name to the whole country, *Industan* or *Hindustan*. It rises in Tibet, is fed by the glaciers of the Himalayas, and flows southwest for 1,900 miles (3,060 km) across Pakistan.

Civilization developed in the valley of the Indus as early as 2500 B.C. The ruins of Mohenjo-Daro (moh-HEN-joh DAHR-oh) show the site of a great city with public buildings and two-story houses of brick, surrounded by a great wall.

The Ganges. The Ganges also rises in the Himalayas and flows eastward across northern India for 1,560 miles (2,500 km) to the flat fields of Bangladesh. There it meets the Brahmaputra to form a vast delta along the Bay of Bengal. A **delta** is a low-lying area at the mouth of a river formed by deposits of silt from the river. The second greatest river of India, the Jumna, joins the Ganges at Allahabad (AL-uh-huh-bad).

These river valleys are the most crowded sections of the country. More villages, more productive irrigated land, and more industries are located along the Ganges and its tributaries than anywhere else in India.

But the Ganges is more than just life-giving water. To Hindus, the Ganges is sacred. Hindus wish to be cremated on its banks and to have their ashes thrown into the river. They bathe in the river with faith that

In Allahabad, where the Jumna River flows into the Ganges, a man at the river's edge waves a cloth in the wind to dry. The broad Ganges stretches into the distance behind him.

their sins, however bad, will be washed away and their souls will be purified. They call it *Ganga Mata*, "Mother Ganges."

The Brahmaputra. The Brahmaputra flows eastward through Tibet and, after spilling through the Himalayas, turns southwest. The river flows for nearly 700 miles (1,125 km) through a region of tea plantations and rice fields in Assam, the far northeastern part of India. From there it flows south into Bangladesh and joins the Ganges as it empties into the Bay of Bengal.

Other Rivers. There are several rivers in the Deccan region: the Narmada (nuhr-MUHD-uh), Tapti (TAHP-tee), Godavari (guh-DAHV-uh-ree), Krishna (KRISH-nuh), and Cauvery (KOH-vuh-ree). Of these, the Narmada, Godavari, and Cauvery are, like the Ganges, sacred rivers. Their banks are lined with Hindu temples and shrines. The Cauvery has been harnessed for irrigation and hydroelectric power. The other rivers of the Deccan are too dry during part of the year to be used for these purposes.

PEOPLE AND LANGUAGES

From earliest times, people from other parts of the world have moved into the subcontinent and found new homes for themselves. They came as travelers, traders, or invaders. They settled down and were absorbed by the peoples who were already there. At the same time, they contributed their own patterns of culture and religion.

A Mixture of Peoples.   Historians disagree about who were the earliest inhabitants of the Indus River valley (3000 B.C.). Many believe that they spoke a **Dravidian** (druh-VID-ee-uhn) language, a language family now found mainly in the south of India. About 1500 B.C., a people called **Aryans** (AIR-ee-uhnz) came to the Indus valley from central Asia. These Caucasian people were nomadic herders. Gradually, the Aryans intermarried with some of the people who were already there. They pushed others southward. Today, Dravidian-speaking peoples dominate southern India from the Vindhya Mountains through the Deccan plateau to Cape Comorin. The northern part of India is inhabited mainly by **Indo-Aryan** speakers.

A Variety of Languages.   India has not one, not two, but sixteen official languages, including **Hindi** (HIN-dee) and English. In addition, 845 minor languages and dialects are spoken. Some of these dialects are related, so that people of different regions are able to understand one another fairly easily. Others are as different as Russian and English.

Pakistan has two official national languages and five official provincial languages. One of the national languages is **Urdu**, which is closely related to Hindi. The other is English. The language of Bangladesh is **Bengali**, which also is spoken in neighboring parts of India.

Like Hindi and Urdu, Bengali is an Indo-Aryan language. The Indo-Aryan languages, most with their own alphabets, are spoken in north and central India, in Bangladesh, and in most of Pakistan. These languages, spoken by more than 80 percent of the people on the subcontinent, derive from an ancient language called **Sanskrit**. Sanskrit is related to the Persian, Greek, Latin, Germanic (including English), Celtic, and Slavic languages of Europe and the Middle East. Many English words are similar to Sanskrit words.

In the eastern part of India, along the borders with Myanmar and China, several Asian languages are spoken. Some of these languages are in the same family as Chinese. Others are related to the languages of Thailand and Vietnam.

The Indian subcontinent is a land where snake charmers entrance deadly cobras, where village girls carry water jars on their heads, and where village women gather to prepare chappattis, or wheat pancakes.

At the western end of the subcontinent, in Pakistan, there are two Iranian languages. These languages, cousins of the Indo-Aryan languages, derive from ancient Persian and are related to Farsi, the modern language of Iran.

In India, the government has faced a serious problem in trying to establish a national language. In 1967 and 1968, riots broke out against an attempt to make Hindi the national language. The government was forced to compromise and permit both English and Hindi.

Most of the Indian states have their own languages. In 1966, the Sikhs (SEEKS), a religious group, created a new state and adopted Punjabi (puhn-JAH-bee) as the official language. All of these state languages, plus English, are recognized as official. However, communications among states or between a state and the national government must be made in English or in Hindi, the two official languages of the central government. English was given this special importance by the Indian constitution. In fact, several years ago, the Indian legislature decided to continue the use of English indefinitely.

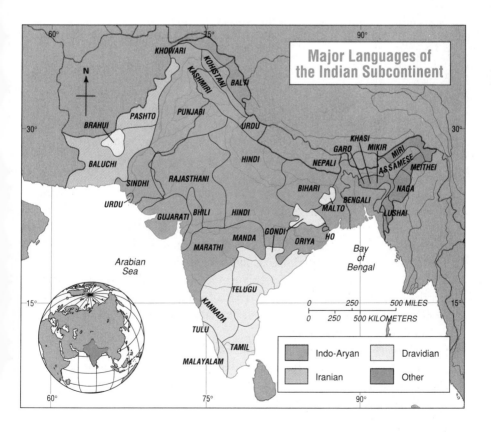

15

Although only 2 percent of the Indian people speak English today, it is the language of commerce, government, and higher education. English is the one language that educated people from different parts of the country can communicate in.

In elementary schools, students learn their own regional language. In junior high school, Hindi is taught in areas where it is not usually spoken. Then English is taught. In many school systems, Sanskrit is also required. Indian students may spend as much as half their time in the study of languages. Most Indians, however, know only their regional language, because the vast majority go only through the lower grades of elementary school.

In India, the diversity of language has been condemned by some Indians as promoting disunity among the peoples of the country. They hope to see English eliminated and Hindi made the one national language. Diversity has been favored by others, particularly government officials, because using the language of the people tends to promote democratic practices between government and the governed. Many educated Indians favor English as a second language, so that they can communicate with the rest of the world.

VILLAGES

More than 80 percent of the people in the subcontinent are farmers who live in villages of 500 to 1,000 people. The size of the some 600,000 villages varies according to the climate, location, and condition of the soil. The villages are the centers of local farming and social activities.

Village Life. The villages are largely self-sufficient, requiring little from outside. Most villagers are farmers. Some provide other services and goods for the entire community. A village usually has a barber and a carpenter, and sometimes a teacher. Traditionally, some families specialize in certain occupations, which have been passed down over the centuries. In the past, these people were paid in food for their services to the farmers. This exchange of goods for services, known as **jajmani** (JAHJ-mah-nee), involved little cash. Jajmani is rapidly disappearing as a money economy replaces it.

Houses are simple. Their walls and floor are made of mud or, increasingly, of bricks. The roof is **thatch**, that is, made of straw, palm leaves, or similar material. Windows and plumbing are rare. Houses are built around courtyards with the center open. The *charpoy* (CHAR-poy),

16

*Many villages depend for their water on the supply from
a well that probably was dug centuries earlier.*

a piece of furniture with many uses, serves as a table, a chair, a bed, a
bench, a stage, or a platform. Also important is a straw mat called a
chatai (CHAH-teye). Chairs or tables are not used in Indian villages.

Cooking utensils are made of wood or pottery, sometimes of brass.
Because of the mild weather, cooking is done and meals are eaten out-
doors or in the courtyard. People squat on their heels and use only their
right hands to eat. In some areas, rice is the main food. In others it is a
wheat pancake called a *chappati* (CHAHP-pah-tee). Mangoes, dates, and
bananas may be part of the meal if they are raised in the neighborhood.

It is against the Hindu religion to eat beef. However, eggs and fish
are sometimes eaten. Muslims may eat beef and lamb, but not pork.
Everyone eats vegetables such as eggplant, peppers, tomatoes, potatoes,
and beans. In most parts of the subcontinent, the main foods are either
wheat or rice, plus milk, *ghee* (liquid butter), and yogurt. Alcohol is forbidden by religion and by law in most of the subcontinent.

Villages often lack some of the conveniences of city living. About a
fifth of them have no electricity, in which case the villagers use small
lanterns or candles. Often there are problems relating to clean water
supply and disposal of sewage. Most villages have wells, and some, of
course, are near rivers.

In some villages there is a doctor. In some others, there is a government nurse and a medical practitioner who is not a fully trained doctor. Small one- or two-room hospitals or clinics provide medical care for
many villages.

17

CITIES

In the subcontinent as a whole there are nearly 50 major cities, and the number is growing. In their most recent censuses, India had 10 cities with populations greater than 1 million, Pakistan had three, and Bangladesh had two. Cities with populations of between 500,000 and 1 million numbered 24 in India, five in Pakistan, and one in Bangladesh. The urban population in India alone is now approaching 235 million.

Delhi. Delhi (DEL-ee) and New Delhi are twin cities located on the Jumna River in northwest India. Their combined population is over 8.3 million. Delhi's old city wall, narrow streets, and **bazaars** (markets or streets of open shops) recall an earlier age. New Delhi, the capital of India, has broad boulevards, wide avenues, gardens, beautiful lawns, pools, modern office buildings, fashionable shops, a racetrack, two golf courses, and two airports. These cities are the leading trade centers of northwest India, as well as the center of political life. Traffic is heavy, and there are a great number of pedestrians and bicyclists.

Calcutta. With its sprawling industrial and residential suburbs, Calcutta (kal-KUHT-uh) is an important center of literature, theater, and music. It is a major seaport and is in the center of India's most highly developed commercial and industrial area. There are more than 11.6 million inhabitants in the metropolitan area, some packed into flimsy, one-room huts. Many homeless people sleep on the sidewalks.

Bombay. Bombay (bahm-BAY), India's largest city, has a population of over 11.7 million. This busy city has the bustling atmosphere of a large Western city with its skyscrapers and big office buildings. Its harbor on the Arabian Sea is the best in the country. Through it flow most of India's imports and exports.

Madras. Madras (muh-DRAS), a city of about 5.7 million residents, is the main trade port for south India. Madras is a center of art, music, and dance. Its many Hindu temples were built during a great period of religious art between A.D. 600 and 1600.

Hyderabad. Located on the Deccan plateau, Hyderabad (HEYE-duh-ruh-bad) with its 3.5 million people is the main city of central India. Islamic rule for centuries has given it a distinctly Islamic appearance with its many mosques and minarets.

18

In Bombay, India's most important commercial center, poor people build temporary homes in the shadow of high-rise office towers.

Karachi. Pakistan's largest city, Karachi (kuh-RAHCH-ee), is a seaport on the Arabian Sea near the mouth of the Indus River. Until the construction of the new capital at Islamabad, it was also Pakistan's capital. It owes its prosperity to its excellent harbor and to the fact that it is the only port for both Pakistan and Afghanistan. It also is Pakistan's commercial and industrial center. Its population is 7.7 million.

Dhaka. The capital of Bangladesh, Dhaka (DAHK-uh), also spelled Dacca, is home to more than 4.2 million people. An important manufacturing center, it also contains many historic buildings and several important educational institutions.

Other cities that have a population of more than 2 million include Bangalore (BANG-guh-lohr), Ahmadabad (AHM-uh-duh-bahd), Poona (POO-nuh), and Kanpur (KAHN-poor) in India, Lahore (luh-HOAR) in Pakistan, and Chittagong (chit-uh-GAHNG) in Bangladesh. India has

19

several important religious centers, including Benares (buh-NAHR-uhs), the most famous holy city of the Hindus, on the Ganges River, and Madurai (mahd-uh-REYE).

AGRICULTURE

Farming is the major occupation in all three countries of the Indian subcontinent. Three-quarters of the people depend on cultivation of the land for their livelihood. The variety of climate, the abundance of rain, the many irrigation projects to store water, and the immense number of people to feed are all factors that explain the importance of farming to the people in the region.

The production of food crops exceeds that of nonfood crops. Among the leading products grown in this region are:

- **Rice.** About a third of the subcontinent's farmlands are devoted to the raising of rice, India's most important crop and the second most important in Bangladesh. Rice is raised in the coastal areas of the peninsula in the south, in the lower Ganges plain, and in Assam, where rainfall is heavy. India is the second-largest rice producer in the world, producing 25 percent of the world's supply. Some rice is imported from Myanmar and the United States, but a larger amount is exported.

- **Wheat and Other Grains.** Wheat, Pakistan's most important crop and India's second most important, is raised in the drier interior and in the northwest. India raises more than 110 million tons a year, making it the world's fourth-largest wheat producer. Farmers in the Punjab get the largest yield per acre of any place in the world. Formerly an importer of wheat, India now raises enough wheat to be able to export it to the nations of the former Soviet Union. Pakistan raises enough wheat for its own needs. In both countries, barley, millet, and corn are also grown in large quantities.

- **Tea.** The chief tea-producing areas are in India along the slopes of the Himalaya and Ghat Mountains, and in northern Bangladesh. India produces 40 percent of the world's tea, and exports most of it.

- **Sugar Cane.** India is fourth among the nations of the world in the production of sugar cane. Sugar cane also is an important crop in both Pakistan and Bangladesh. It is raised in the irrigated lands of the upper Indus River and in the foothills of the Himalayas.

20

- **Cotton.** Cotton is an Indian discovery. The cotton plant was first farmed there about 2500 B.C. The chief cotton-growing region in India is in the Deccan. India is among the largest cotton-producing countries in the world. Indian cotton has short fibers because, during the growing season, the Deccan region does not get enough rain for the cotton fibers to grow long before they are picked. Cotton cloth made from short-fiber cotton is not as fine as U.S. cotton cloth, but it is widely used throughout India and other Asian countries. Much cotton also is grown in Pakistan, where it is the nation's most important export.

- **Jute.** Jute is a plant from which comes a coarse fiber that is made into burlap bags, rope, twine, and carpets. In Bangladesh, it is the principal crop and the most important export. The fertile soil, heavy rainfall, abundant sunshine, and large number of available workers have helped make this an important crop. It also is raised in neighboring parts of India. Much U.S. cotton is wrapped in burlap made in the subcontinent. Burlap is a leading export of India because, though the jute is raised in Bangladesh, the cloth is made in India.

India also raises peanuts, which are used for cattle feed and the manufacture of peanut oil. Most of the world's **shellac** is supplied by India. Shellac is a wood-finishing product made from a substance deposited by insects on trees. Coffee, nuts, and spices (cinnamon, ginger, pepper) are grown along the Malabar coast.

In Bangladesh, the ever-increasing population raises serious food problems. In India and Pakistan, where population is also increasingly rapidly, food production in recent years has managed to keep pace. Many families have tiny farms and must use most of the food they grow for their own needs. Most of the milk, vegetables, fruit, and grain grown on the farm is used on the farm.

In the past, outdated farming methods kept production down. Farm tools often were less efficient than those used elsewhere. Seeds may not have been carefully chosen, so that poor seed was mixed with richer types, resulting in poor yields. Lack of fertilizer to restore the tired soil also contributed to poor yields in some areas.

In many of these aspects of Indian farming, however, there has been significant improvement in recent years. Seeds and fertilizers, in particular, have improved. The change has been so great that it is referred to as the "Green Revolution." India and Pakistan are now able to raise enough food for their people, and the growth in food produc-

21

tion has kept ahead of the increase in population. In the ten years from 1980 to 1990, for example, production of rice, wheat, and other grains in India increased at an average rate of 5 percent a year. This increase occurred despite below-average yields in two of the ten years because of failed monsoons.

When the monsoon does not provide the water necessary to raise crops, the people of the subcontinent once were faced with hunger and famine. In 1965 and 1966, when the monsoon rains failed, thousands would have died if the United States and other nations had not sent in millions of tons of wheat. Since the 1970s, surpluses from earlier years have made such foreign aid unnecessary.

Animals. Although most Hindus do not eat beef, there are more than 200 million cattle and buffalo in India, more than in any other country in the world. These animals are protected from being slaughtered. However, they are the main source of milk and of fuel for cooking. Because it is against the law to cut down trees for fuel, farm families burn cow dung for fuel. Bullocks are used as work animals on the farms. After the animals die, their skins are made into leather, a major export.

A scooter driver dodges a group of cows basking on a busy street in downtown New Delhi. More than 200 million cattle roam India's streets, unhindered by traffic.

Pakistan and Bangladesh have about 40 million cattle between them. In these countries, the animals can be slaughtered, and beef and veal are important products.

The subcontinent's 138 million goats and 90 million sheep are concentrated in India and Pakistan. Both produce quantities of wool, including the famous cashmere. *Cashmere* is an alternative spelling of *Kashmir,* the name of a northern region of India and Pakistan.

In the forests and streams, there are monkeys, baboons, deer, wild boar, elephants, tigers, leopards, crocodiles, and alligators. There are also poisonous snakes, such as the cobra. Many of these animals are now considered to be endangered species. Tigers, once a constant danger to jungle villagers, are nearly extinct and are protected by the government. Elephants, once trained to do many heavy tasks and still used in the lumber industry, are also an endangered species.

NATURAL AND INDUSTRIAL RESOURCES

The Indian subcontinent has large deposits of several important minerals. Some of these are exported, while others serve as the basis for the subcontinent's growing industries.

Minerals.   India's rich mineral reserves make it a leading producer of iron ore. India mines about 70 million tons of coal a year. Almost all of it goes to the railroads and to the steel plants. India ranks third in the mining of manganese, which is used in making steel. The Tata steel plant at Jamshedpur (JAHM-shed-poor), in the northeast, is the largest in India. It produces almost one million tons a year. India ranks as the third largest steel-producing country in Asia, after Japan and the People's Republic of China.

India has a rich supply of other useful minerals, such as ilmenite (for the metal titanium), bauxite (to make aluminum), monazite (from which uranium and thorium are derived), and talc. It is the world's largest supplier of mica, a kind of mineral used in the manufacture of electronic products. Its gold mines are among the richest in the world. Diamonds, sapphires, and emeralds are also mined.

Pakistan has large deposits of coal and of chromite, the chief ore of the metal chromium. It has smaller quantities of many other minerals. Bangladesh has few mineral resources.

Although some oil has been found in India and Pakistan, it is far from enough for either country's needs, so that oil is the largest single

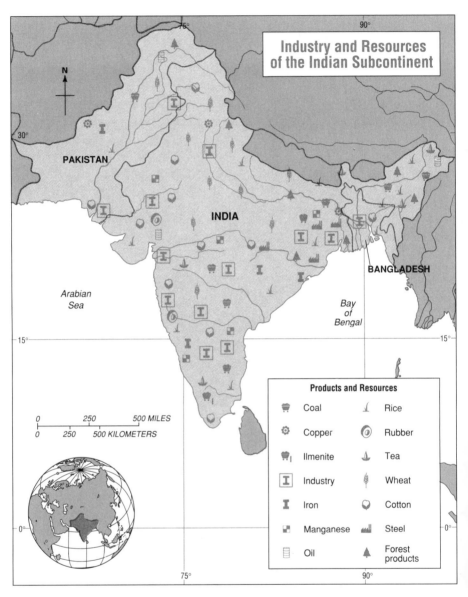

Industry and Resources of the Indian Subcontinent

N

30°

PAKISTAN

INDIA

BANGLADESH

Arabian
Sea

Bay
of
Bengal

15°   15°

0   250   500 MILES
0   250   500 KILOMETERS

Products and Resources

🛒	Coal	⌿	Rice
⚙	Copper	◎	Rubber
🛒ₗ	Ilmenite	⚓	Tea
I	Industry	🌾	Wheat
I	Iron	◗	Cotton
▪	Manganese	▦	Steel
▤	Oil	▲	Forest products

75°   90°

import of both countries. The subcontinent also lacks such important minerals as copper, tin, and nickel, which are needed in modern industries, and it has little lead and zinc. Future exploration of the country may uncover these or other natural resources.

Forests. Forests cover 150 million square miles (389 million square km) of India, about one-fifth of the land. On the lower slopes of the

Himalayas there are fir, spruce, cedar, and blue pine trees. Below this area of cone-bearing trees, forests of oak, chestnut, and walnut can be found. There are forests of exotic woods such as sandalwood, satinwood, teak, acacia, and ebony, used for decorative objects. The timber is used for building purposes and for making charcoal, paper, matches, and plywood.

The number of mills for processing wood products is growing. In addition, the forests yield large supplies of resins, gums, essential oils, and tanning materials.

Water Power. India and Pakistan are potentially rich in hydroelectric power because of their many rivers. Large dams for irrigation, flood control, and electric power have been built, and miles of transmission lines have been laid. Electricity is now used for many large factories, and about 80 percent of India's villages are now electrified. The amount of electricity produced from water power is still small, however, in comparison to these countries' needs.

India produces about 225 million kilowatt hours of electricity per year, Pakistan about 28 million, and Bangladesh about 5 million. These figures compare with nearly 3 billion kilowatt hours per year for the United States. About one-fourth of India's electricity is hydroelectric, as is about one-half of Pakistan's. India and Pakistan are hoping to develop the use of nuclear power to supply electricity cheaply.

Transportation. The subcontinent of India has the largest railroad system in Asia and the fourth largest in the world. There are more than 45,600 miles (73,500 km) of track in the three nations. The railroads carry most of the subcontinent's freight and a large part of its passenger traffic, but there still are not enough trains. The operation of the railroads is complicated by the use of four different gauges (track widths).

Automobiles and trucks are becoming more common, but the high cost of gasoline limits their usefulness. There are more than 1.3 million miles (2 million km) of roads, of which nearly 560,000 miles (900,000 km) are hard-surfaced or concrete. The rest are dirt. Most local transportation is by oxcart, bicycle, or foot.

India has 92 airports, local and international. Pakistan has 32, and Bangladesh ten. Air India, Air Pakistan, and Bangladesh Airways offer overseas service, as do many foreign airlines. International airports are at Bombay, Calcutta, Madras, and Delhi in India, Karachi in Pakistan, and Dhaka in Bangladesh. The flight by jet from New York to one of these cities takes about 17 hours.

25

In Bombay, a gasoline tank pulled by an ox crosses a broad street in front of a waiting fleet of taxis.

Water transportation is important in coastal areas and on parts of the Ganges and Brahmaputra rivers in Bangladesh and northeastern India. Most other rivers cannot be depended on for transportation because they dry up during the hot months preceding the arrival of the monsoon. The large amounts of water removed from the rivers for irrigation further reduce the water level of these rivers.

Manufacturing. India is the tenth largest manufacturing nation of the world. Heavy industry includes steel mills, aluminum and cement factories, and chemical, fertilizer, and machine tool plants. Textile manufacturing is the largest industry. Large mills turn out fabrics made of cotton and jute. Other plants produce cigarettes, sugar, vegetable oils, and articles made of rubber or leather.

26

A worker in a steel mill separates waste material from molten iron. India is now one of the world's major steel producers.

In Pakistan, the largest industries are food processing, textiles, and chemicals. Jute-processing mills are the main industry in Bangladesh.

The largest part of manufactured merchandise and the largest number of workers work in cottage industries. A **cottage industry** is one whose goods are produced by people working at home. These home workshops hand-loom cotton, silk, and wool and process most agricultural products. Highly skilled artisans work in brass, copper, silver, gold, and exotic woods to make artistic objects for export.

27

REVIEWING THE CHAPTER

I. Building Your Vocabulary

In your notebook, write the word that matches the definition.

subcontinent   alluvium   monsoon   Sanskrit
Dravidians   Aryans   Hindi

1. People who migrated to the Indus River Valley around 1500 B.C.

2. a large landmass that is part of a larger continent but separated from it by natural barriers

3. one of India's two official languages

4. the earliest inhabitants of the Indus River Valley, who now dominate the southern part of India

5. ancient language of India that is related to many other languages of Europe and the Middle East

6. topsoil washed down by rivers from higher elevations and deposited on lower ground

7. wind that brings the rainy season when it blows from the ocean

II. Understanding the Facts

In your notebook, write the numbers from 1 to 6. Write the letter of the correct answer to each question next to its number.

1. What mountains separate the Malabar Coast from the Deccan plateau?
   a. Western Ghats   b. Eastern Ghats   c. Himalayas

2. Which of the following nations is *not* located on the Indian subcontinent?
   a. Tibet   b. Pakistan   c. Bangladesh

3. Where does India rank in population among the nations of the world?
   a. tenth   b. second   c. first

4. What determines the seasons in India and Bangladesh?
   a. the monsoon   b. the elevation   c. the ocean currents
5. Which river is sacred to Hindus?
   a. the Indus   b. the Brahmaputra   c. the Ganges
6. What language is understood by educated people throughout India?
   a. Hindi   b. English   c. Sanskrit

III. Thinking It Through

In your notebook, write the numbers from 1 to 6. Write the letter of the correct conclusion to each sentence next to its number.

1. The Himalayas are important to the Indian subcontinent because:
   a. the main rivers of the subcontinent rise there.
   b. the mineral wealth of the subcontinent is located there.
   c. they divide India and Pakistan.
   d. they divide Pakistan and Bangladesh.

2. The strongest reason for the dense population of the Lowland plain is:
   a. the continual deposit of rich topsoil by the rivers.
   b. the absence of wild animals.
   c. the desire to be near to the sacred Ganges River.
   d. the temperate climate.

3. The most accurate description of the Indian monsoon is:
   a. a seasonal rain that falls in March, April, and May.
   b. a wind that reverses direction, causing a rainy season from May through October and a dry season from November through April.
   c. seasonal flooding in northeast India.
   d. occasional rainstorms caused by shifting winds.

4. The Ganges River and its tributaries are important to India for each of the following reasons *except*:
   a. they bring deposits of rich topsoil from the mountains.
   b. they provide a method of transportation.
   c. their waters can be used for irrigation.
   d. India's earliest civilization developed on their shores.

29

5. Which statement best describes a consequence of the many languages spoken in India?
   a. Communication among Indians from different regions can be difficult.
   b. Most Indians now speak and read English.
   c. India's many languages help make its government democratic.
   d. Most educated Indians now speak Hindi.

6. Rice is grown in India in the coastal areas of the south, in the lower Ganges plain, and in Assam because:
   a. rice requires a constant supply of water.
   b. rice requires large fields with moderate rainfall.
   c. rice needs the cool night temperature of mountain slopes.
   d. rice needs heavy mechanized equipment.

DEVELOPING CRITICAL THINKING SKILLS

1. Compare the topography of northern India to that of southern India.
2. Why are the Himalayas an important feature of the Indian subcontinent?
3. Why is the Ganges River called "Mother Ganges"?
4. What problems does India's diversity of languages create?
5. What is the connection between the diet of Hindus and their religious beliefs?

INTERPRETING A MAP

The map shows where the people of the Indian subcontinent live. Use it and the maps facing page 1 and on pages 7, 8, 9, 15, and 24 to answer the questions.

1. Compare the population map to the map facing page 1. Along what river valley is the population over 500 persons per square mile? Which two countries claim territory in the river valley?
2. Compare the population map and the map on page 7. What is the general climate of the least populated regions of the Indian subcontinent?

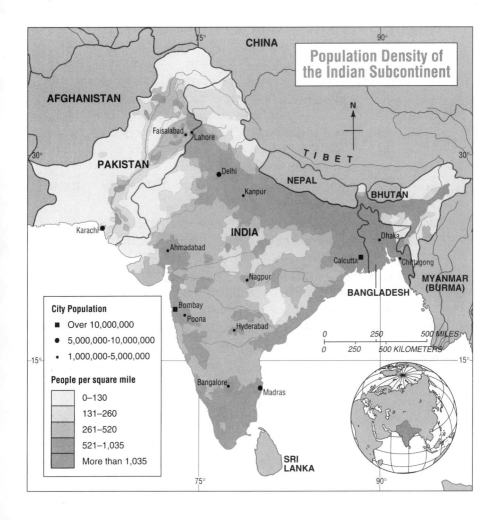

Population Density of the Indian Subcontinent

City Population
- ■ Over 10,000,000
- ● 5,000,000–10,000,000
- • 1,000,000–5,000,000

People per square mile
- 0–130
- 131–260
- 261–520
- 521–1,035
- More than 1,035

3. Compare the population map to the map on page 15. Describe the population density of the Hindi-speaking regions of India. Describe the population density of the Bengali-speaking regions of the Indian subcontinent.

4. Using the maps on page 7 and 24, make a generalization about the kinds of climate suitable for growing rice, for growing wheat, and for growing cotton.

5. What part of the subcontinent has the fewest large cities? Use other maps in the chapter to explain why there are fewer large cities in this area.

ENRICHMENT AND EXPLORATION

1. Find out about the wild animals of the Indian subcontinent. Consult such references as encyclopedias, geographical encyclopedias, and books about wildlife to find out where each of the following creatures lives: Indian elephant, bonnet monkey, leopard, gaur, nilgai, Indian rhinoceros, Indian cobra, Bengal tiger, black buck, Sarus crane, Indian gavial. Then draw a rough map of India on a sheet of paper and indicate where each of the animals or reptiles lives. You may make a key for your map, write the names of the species directly on the map, or use pictures on the map.

2. Plan a two-week vacation to India, Pakistan, or Bangladesh. Consult travel guides in the local library and/or visit a local travel agent. Make a travel plan that answers the following questions: What cities and sites will you visit? (List at least five.) How will you reach them? (Use maps to see if you can use railroads and if there are paved roads to travel by car.) You will want to bring home a souvenir or gift from each of the places you visit. What are the handicrafts or specialities that you might purchase in each area?

3. Use an Indian cookbook to plan an Indian meal. Make a list of ingredients that are common in the United States. Make a list of the ingredients you might have difficulty finding. With the help of a parent or teacher, prepare one or two Indian dishes such as a curry, basmati rice, or cucumber raita.

4. Prepare a five-minute talk on one of the following topics:
   a. the conquest of Mount Everest
   b. the monsoons—curse or blessing
   c. Sanskrit—the root of many languages
   d. the steel industry of India

2 The Religions of India

The people of the subcontinent include followers of a number of religions. Of these, Hinduism and Islam have the largest numbers of followers. The beliefs of these religions, and the conflicts among their followers, play an important part in government and society on the subcontinent. Other religions, including several that originated in India, have smaller numbers of followers.

HINDUISM

Of the many religions in the subcontinent, the largest single religion is Hinduism (HIN-doo-iz-uhm). There are about 700 million Hindus in India, or about 82 percent of the population. There also are about 14 million Hindus in Bangladesh and about 1 million in Pakistan.

Hinduism is more than a religion. It is a way of life. It provides a guide for everything a Hindu does or may do from the moment of birth to the moment of death. Hinduism is a philosophy. It explains the moral obligations of people and their duties in their various roles of husband or wife, parent, family provider, or ruler.

Hinduism is also a social system. Its many **castes** and **subcastes**, based on the principle of purity and pollution, divide people into groups according to birth and occupation. With these divisions come rules and regulations concerning social relations among members of the same caste and with those of different castes.

Unlike other great religions, Hinduism has no one founder, like Jesus or Muhammad. It has no central authority, like the Roman Catholic pope, or any organization for working together, like that of the Presbyterian Church. It has no main religious book, like the Bible or the Koran, and no fixed creed.

Hindus have a variety of beliefs and practices. Some believe that God is everywhere—in every rock, every tree, every particle of matter—and because people are different they need different ways of approaching God. They believe in a Supreme Being who is called Brahman (BRAH-muhn). But Brahman takes many forms and has different functions. This has led to the worship of various **deities**, or gods and goddesses, many of whom are local or village deities.

The important deities are Vishnu (VISH-noo), the preserver; Siva (SEE-vuh), the destroyer (of ignorance and evil); and Devi (DAY-vee), the mother goddess. Hinduism is a tolerant religion, accepting many other beliefs and adding new beliefs to its ancient ones. As a result, it is difficult for other religions to gain a foothold in India.

If Hinduism does not have a Bible or a Koran, where then may one find its religious beliefs and practices written down?

Sources of Hinduism.   Hinduism is one of the oldest faiths among the great religions of the world. Its basic ideas spring from the Indus Valley civilization and the Indo-European Aryans when they invaded about 1500 B.C. Much later, its major concepts were written down in a language called Sanskrit. The scriptures revered by all Hindus are the *Vedas* (VAY-duhz), or collections of sacred psalms, prayers, magic charms, and chants. The most famous veda is the *Rig-Veda*. It is the oldest known religious text in Hinduism, dating from about 1400 B.C.

In the *Rig-Veda* is found a "Hymn of Creation," in which a universal spirit is mentioned. Here is part of the hymn:

> Darkness was hidden in a deeper darkness;
> This All was as a sea without dimensions,
> The void still held unformed what was potential,
> Until the power of Warmth produced the sole One . . . .
> Whether he made the world or did not make it,
> He knows whence this creation came, he only
> Who in the highest heaven guards and watches;
> He knows indeed, but then, perhaps he knows not!

Another source of information about Hinduism is the *Brahmanas*. These are collections of rituals and ceremonies, composed in the 8th and 7th centuries B.C. The *Upanishads* (oo-PAN-ih-shadz) are commentaries on the individual soul and the origin of the universe. They were written between 700 and 200 B.C. The *Law Book of Manu* (250 B.C.) regulates social and daily life in terms of religion.

Hindu temples are known for the elaborate carvings on their outside walls, as in this temple at Mysore, in southern India.

Great Stories. Great epic masterpieces tell us much about Hinduism. The two most important are the *Mahabharata* (muh-HAH-BAH-ruh-tuh), whose approximately 200,000 lines make it the longest poem ever written, and the *Ramayana* (rah-MAH-yuh-nuh).

The *Mahabharata* was written over a period of several centuries. It has had a great influence on Hindu character and conduct. The most famous section of the long poem is the *Bhagavad-Gita* (BUHG-uh-vuhd GEE-tah), written about 200 B.C., which summarizes the major beliefs of Hinduism.

Statues to the Hindu gods and goddesses are among the Indian subcontinent's great works of art. The statue of Brahman, at right, is more than a thousand years old.

Another important god in the Hindu religion is Vishnu, the preserver (left).

The *Bhagavad-Gita* tells the story of Arjuna (AHR-joo-nuh), the perfect warrior, on the eve of an important battle between rival armies. Arjuna is unhappy because in the army opposing him are many of his friends and relatives. He does not want to kill them, but he does not want to lose the fight, either.

He turns for advice to his charioteer, who reveals himself as Krishna, one of the deities. Krishna explains to the warrior that the purpose of life is to know God. This can be accomplished by meditation, by good conduct in this world, and by loving devotion. God may be reached by human efforts, which will lead to truth and salvation. Krishna also speaks to Arjuna about the duties of all the people, the organization of society, the obligation of each person to do his or her duty, and the idea that a person should act according to one's principles regardless of consequences. The story ends with Arjuna victorious in the battle.

The high moral tone of Krishna's advice has had a profound influence on Hindus throughout the centuries. Mohandas Gandhi (MOH-han-dahs GAHN-dee), of whom you will read later in this book, called the *Bhagavad-Gita* a "dictionary of conduct," from which he drew the inspiration for his doctrine of nonviolence.

The *Ramayana* tells the story of the god Rama (RAH-muh) and his wife Sita. Rama loses his throne because his father, King Dasratha (DAHS-rah-tah), keeps a promise made to his queen whereby the throne would go to Rama's stepbrother. For years Rama and Sita travel throughout India, having many adventures.

One day Sita is kidnapped by the evil king Ravana (RAH-vah-nah) of Ceylon. She finally is rescued by brave Rama, his loyal brother Lakshamana (LAHK-shah-mah-nah), and the daring Hanuman (hah-NOO-mahn), the monkey general, and his monkey army. Hanuman sets Ravana's palace on fire by lighting his own tail and swinging from one part of the palace to another. It is because of the great help of the monkey army in this story that monkeys are considered sacred by Hindus.

After a long exile, Rama returns to his kingdom to assume his rightful place on the throne. Sita returns with him to rule as his queen, but later is banished so that Rama's reputation as a fair ruler will not be questioned. A different version of the story tells how Rama and Sita lived happily together for many years as rulers of the kingdom.

To generations of Hindus, Rama and Sita have shown how human beings should behave. The loyalty, love, devotion, obedience, and sense of duty in this often-repeated story have been an inspiration to Hindu children.

Chief Religious Ideas. Three main concepts in Hinduism provide unifying elements in a religion that tolerates so many differences in social structure and the worship of so many gods and goddesses. These three concepts are **reincarnation, karma,** and **dharma.**

- **Reincarnation.** The Hindu religion teaches that a person's soul (*atman*) never dies; only the body does. Upon death, the soul moves into the body of another living thing—a person or an animal. This belief in the transmigration of souls is called *samsara* (sum-SAH-ruh). The soul is reborn in another body, then goes again through death and rebirth in an effort to achieve *moksha* (MOK-shah), the final state of salvation and freedom from the life-death cycle.

  Living things are not all equal, according to this teaching. A crawling insect, a four-legged animal, a bird, a person—all are different rungs on the ladder reaching toward *moksha*. A soul moves up or down on this ladder according to its *karma*.

- **Karma.** *Karma* (KAHR-muh) is the belief that a person's actions in life determine his or her future state in the next rebirth. Good behavior will bring promotion to a higher level. Bad behavior will bring demotion to a lower level—to a lower caste or perhaps even to the level of an insect.

  The word *karma* means "deed." A person's present state is the result of all previous acts. Present and future acts determine the person's future state. A person cannot escape the result of his or her actions. If a person or an animal lives a good life, according to his or her *dharma* (DUHR-muh), the soul will be rewarded by being reincarnated in the next rebirth into a higher-ranking human or animal. Good behavior and a good life are determined by *dharma*.

- **Dharma.** This is the set of rules that must be followed by each living thing if it desires to be promoted in its next reincarnation. This "path of righteousness" is different for each living thing, depending on one's age, sex, and caste. A person's *dharma* includes obligations and duties within the family and the society into which he or she was born. As Krishna advised Arjuna in the *Bhagavad-Gita*, "It is better to do one's own *dharma* poorly than to do another's well." Hindus, therefore, are offered the hope that they may determine their futures in the next life by their actions in their present lives.

Religious Practices.   Most Hindus follow strict rituals of washing and cleanliness, faithful worship at shrines, and severe dietary laws.

- Hindus from all over India spend months making pilgrimages on foot to holy cities like Benares.
- Hindus wash their hands and feet in pools before praying daily at the many temples. They bathe in sacred rivers like the Ganges.
- When a person dies, he or she is cremated the same day. A male is wrapped in white cloth, a female in red cloth. The eldest son walks around the pyre three times and prays before starting the fire. In most cities the places where cremations take place, called Burning Ghats, are holy places.
- The Hindus consider all life sacred, especially cattle, which may not be slaughtered. India has more cattle than any other country. Because of their belief that cattle are sacred, most Hindus are vegetarians. They do not eat meat. Some cattle are used for plowing, and the cows for milking. Many others belong to no one and roam the streets of villages, even of cities, and go unharmed.

Hindu pilgrims bathe in the Ganges River at the holy city of Benares. The waters of the Ganges, to Hindus the most sacred of rivers, are believed to purify the bather.

The Caste System. The caste system has been closely related to Hinduism for 3,000 years. The system may have originated in the Indus Valley civilization, or it may have been introduced by the Aryans who invaded India about 1500 B.C. These conquering Aryans probably forced the Dravidians to become their servants and perform the work needed to maintain society. Thus, the caste system may have originated as a way of defining social and economic distinctions.

In the caste system, all people were divided into groups according to birth, based on purity and pollution. There were five main castes and more than 3,000 subcastes. The main castes were:

- **Brahmans** (BRAH-muhnz), or priestly class and cultured elite;
- **Kshatriyas** (kuh-SHAT-ree-yuhz), or warrior class and ruling aristocracy;
- **Vaisyas** (VEYES-yuhz), or farmer, professional, and artisan class;
- **Shudras** (SHOO-druhz), or servant class;
- **Untouchables**, or lowest class, called variously "outcastes," "scheduled castes," and, by Mohandas Gandhi, *harijans* (HAH-ree-jahnz), or "children of God."

A person was born into his or her caste and remained in it throughout life. Born a street cleaner's son, a man must be a street cleaner; born a street cleaner's daughter, a woman must marry a street cleaner. A merchant's son must be a merchant, and his daughter, a merchant's wife. Perhaps, in a later life, a person who has followed his or her *dharma* conscientiously well might become something better.

Each caste had its own code of behavior, duties, and responsibilities. This code influenced the education, occupation, diet, marriage, and social privileges of every member in the caste.

Under the caste system, everyone knew what was expected. The tailor, the carpenter, the blacksmith, the farmer, the teacher—everyone's life was laid out. If a person was dissatisfied with his or her place in life, he or she could hope that in the next reincarnation the soul would be promoted to a higher subcaste, or even to a higher caste.

The Untouchables. Prior to Mohandas Gandhi, the Untouchables were regarded as the lowest of the castes. Indeed, they were "outcastes"—they did not even belong to the system. More than 40 million Untouchables were considered unfit to worship in Hindu temples, were prohibited from using public roads, and could not let their children play with the children of any other caste. They were limited to the lowest occupations, such as street cleaners or tanners. Since the skins of the sacred cattle could not be handled by a caste Hindu, this job was left to the non-caste people.

The lot of the millions of Untouchables has improved considerably in the last 50 years. Gandhi began a campaign to raise their status and accepted them as his pupils. The Indian constitution (1950) outlawed untouchability and made discrimination against any citizen on the grounds of religion, race, caste, sex, or place of birth punishable by law. In 1968, a new law provided that 22 percent of government jobs were to go to ex-Untouchables, now officially called **Scheduled Castes**. In 1989, a government commission recommended that the number of reserved government jobs be doubled. Many Scheduled Caste members have entered politics, and throughout India *harijans* have come to active political leadership. Yet even in politics, where the votes of the Scheduled Castes are important, great discrimination remains.

Weakening Caste Lines. Today the caste system is still practiced in India. Custom and tradition change slowly, although many factors are weakening the system. These include:

- The great increase in educational opportunities for more and more Indians, regardless of caste, and the improvement of status due to the availability of better jobs;

- The increasing movement of people from villages to cities with large populations, where caste lines are blurred, castes mingle, and caste restrictions have less importance;

- The constitutional changes favoring Untouchables; also, the universal suffrage law, which gives all people, male and female, regardless of caste membership, the equal right to vote;

- The leadership of people like Mohandas Gandhi, who fought discrimination; Indira Gandhi (no relation), who was the first woman to become Indian Prime Minister; and others, all of whom are against caste discrimination;

- The growth of industry, with increasing need for jobs that cut across caste lines.

Continuing Caste Strength. The caste system has not, however, completely disappeared from India. It will take many, many years before all

CASE STUDY:
Caste in the Villages

The following selection is taken from a book written by an Indian woman journalist. It was written about 15 years after Indian independence and 12 years after untouchability had been abolished.

> In the same village I walked into the house of a grey-bearded Sikh peasant. Though not too impressive or clean, his house is big. In the courtyard two beautiful big bullocks are standing with a bright yellow cloth covering their backs. Cotton is lying on the ground to dry. The man has sufficient land, and according to him everything is fine. He is not a refugee and his fortunes therefore have not suffered any recent upheaval. Just then a woman comes in, wearing a blue salwar and kameez (baggy trousers and a long skirt). A warm shawl covers her head and part of the face. Slim, light of skin and with buck teeth and dirty hands she is obviously very angry. Mistaking me perhaps for an emissary of the government, she lets forth a torrent of complaints: not only is the present administration not doing anything for the zemindars [landlords], but it is positively conspiring against them.
>
> "But why are you so angry?" I ask mildly. . . .
>
> "Why?" she repeats. "The government has given land to Harijans [Untouchables] in this village. The result is that they will not do our work. And now I, a Jat woman," (with heavy emphasis on the word *Jat*), "I have to dirty my hands and do this work of making cowdung cakes. Is this a Jat's work?"
>
> "But don't you want the condition of Harijans also to improve?" I ask.
>
> "Why should it?" is the forceful reply with the full weight of conviction behind it. "Harijans were born to do menial [fit for servants] jobs. God made them such, and they should be allowed to continue as such. Am I meant for this—do I deserve it?" and she holds out her dirty hands to invite sympathy.

Kusum Nair, *Blossoms in the Dust.* New York: Praeger, 1961, pages 109–110.

1. In this section of India, the Jats are well off. Why would these people feel threatened by the improvement in Untouchables' lives?

2. What methods can a country use to make such changes more acceptable to its people?

42

traces of it vanish. Caste is still strong in the villages, and most of the people of India live in villages. There, change is slow. The influences of education and industrialization have only begun to be felt in villages.

For example, caste is still the most important consideration when marriage is being planned. Many Indians consider the caste system an essential part of Hinduism. Thus, a Hindu's acceptance of the religious doctrines of *karma* and *dharma* includes the obligations of caste membership. India is slow to change, and nowhere as slow as in its attitude toward caste.

ISLAM

The second great religion of the Indian subcontinent, after Hinduism, is **Islam** (IS-lahm), with more than 300 million followers on the subcontinent. Followers of Islam call themselves **Muslims** (MUHZ-luhmz). Slightly over two-thirds of the subcontinent's Muslims are in the mainly Islamic republics of Pakistan and Bangladesh. The rest are in India, where they make up about 11.4 percent of the population.

The Five Pillars of Islam. *Islam,* an Arabic word, means both "submission to God" and "peace." It is the religious faith preached by the Arab prophet Muhammad (moo-HAM-uhd), who lived during the 7th century A.D. Islam is at the same time a religion and a way of life. It is based on five main duties, known as the "Five Pillars of Islam." These are the things that a Muslim is expected to do, listed in order of importance:

- *Shahada,* or statement of faith. Muslims declare that "There is no God but God, and Muhammad is is the messenger of God."

- *Salat,* or prayer. All Muslims are required to pray at five different times of the day, always facing Mecca as they kneel.

- *Sawm,* or fasting. The Islamic month of Ramadan is celebrated as the month when God revealed himself to Muhammad. Throughout Ramadan, Muslims fast from dawn to dusk.

- *Zakat,* or charity. Muslims believe that the less fortunate among them must be helped, and they are expected to give a portion of their income to charity.

- The *hajj,* or pilgrimage. Once in his or her life, every Muslim who is able is supposed to make a pilgrimage to Mecca. Mecca, in Saudi Arabia, is Muhammad's birthplace and the holiest city of Islam.

43

A group of women gather before a mosque in Delhi. Five times each day, Muslims are summoned to prayer by criers in the minarets, the tall towers at the corners of the mosque.

The Koran. Islam's holy book is the Koran (kuh-RAN), the collection of Muhammad's revelations. Muslims believe the Koran to be the word of God revealed to Muhammad through the angel Gabriel. These teachings were not written down while Muhammad was alive, but were memorized and recited. After his death, these sayings were collected, written down, and organized into the Koran. *Koran* in Arabic means "recite," which was God's first command to Muhammad. It is organized into 144 *suras*, or chapters.

The Spread of Islam. After Muhammad's death in 632, the religion spread rapidly along the shores of North Africa, into Spain and Portugal, and across the Asian mainland. It first came into India in the 8th century. There was a second and greater wave in the 13th century. The Mogul Empire, which reached its peak in the 16th century, brought Islamic rule to much of the subcontinent.

The greatest concentrations of Muslims in the subcontinent are in the Indus valley of Pakistan, where Islam has been important since the 8th century, and in the eastern province of Bengal, now Bangledesh, where many people converted to Islam in the 16th century. Because Islam emphasizes that all believers are equal before God, it appealed to many in Bengal as an escape from the caste system.

OTHER RELIGIONS

The subcontinent is home to followers of several other religions besides Hinduism and Islam. Three of these religions, Jainism, Buddhism, and Sikhism, originated there. Christianity and Parsiism, like Islam, were introduced to India from countries to the west. Most followers of these religions live in India, with few in Pakistan and Bangladesh.

Jainism. As early as the 6th century B.C., some Hindus rebelled against early Hindu practices. They found animal sacrifices, which were a part of Hinduism at that time, to be particularly distasteful. In Magadha, after twelve years of reflection, a religious teacher who was called *Mahavira* ("great hero") and *Jaina* ("victor") proclaimed himself the prophet of a new religion. This religion, Jainism (JEYEN-iz-uhm), has about 3.2 million members today.

Jains (JEYENZ) are taught strong self-control. They vow to kill no living thing, to tell no lies, and to steal nothing. They carry their most important religious belief, nonviolence toward all living things (*ahimsa* [uh-HIM-suh]), to unusual lengths, such as trying to avoid stepping on insects.

Lay members of this religion live in the large cities of western India, are usually merchants, and often are wealthy. They believe strongly in education and are strict vegetarians. Although relatively few in number, they have had considerable influence upon other Indians.

Buddhism. One of the great religions of the world, Buddhism (BOO-diz-uhm) developed in India in the 6th and 5th centuries B.C. It spread throughout the subcontinent, then moved across frontiers to other Asian countries, including China, Japan, Vietnam, and Sri Lanka. Because many of its major beliefs were absorbed by Hinduism, it lost the importance that it once had in India, the land of its origin. Today there are about 4.7 million Buddhists in India. Few live in Pakistan or Bangladesh.

The founder of this religion was Siddhartha Gautama (sid-DAHR-tuh GAH-oo-tah-mah). Gautama (563–487 B.C.) was born of a royal family in a small kingdom at the foothills of the Himalaya Mountains. His father surrounded him with every luxury and shielded him from all unpleasant things. His life was changed when he was about 30 years old. One day, while riding outside the palace, he saw a bent, tired old man for the first time in his life. He was shocked to realize that all people grow old. When he saw crippled, diseased, and dead people, he realized that life was not all pleasure. These sights troubled him and set him thinking about the meaning of life.

He left his beautiful wife and newborn son and wandered for six years throughout the country. As he traveled, he sought answers to his questions about the behavior of people and the meaning of life. The answers came to him suddenly, as an inspiration, and made him the "Enlightened One," or Buddha.

A statue of the Buddha and his disciples at Sarnath, in northern India near Benares. It was at Sarnath that the Buddha first taught. The sculpture dates from the 2nd century B.C.

Buddha spent the next 40 years teaching his beliefs. The secret of life's meaning was to be found in the Four Noble Truths:

- Life is full of pain and suffering.
- Desires cause this suffering.
- By putting an end to desire, a person can end suffering.
- There is a way to end desire.

In other words, desire for things, not the lack of the possessions themselves, is the root of unhappiness.

The way to eliminate desire was through the Eightfold Path: (1) right knowledge of the cause and ending of suffering; (2) high and worthy intentions; (3) kind, frank, and truthful speech; (4) right conduct; (5) right livelihood that does not injure any living thing; (6) the right effort to train oneself; (7) right mindfulness; (8) right meditation.

Each person, Buddha taught, could attain *nirvana* (nihr-VAH-nuh). He preached many sermons, urging his followers to avoid any kind of extreme action, to tell the truth at all times, to avoid violence and the killing of living things, human or animal. He taught that everyone can escape the evils in this life by good deeds and pure thoughts and by giving up worldly desires.

In Buddhism, there is no Supreme Being who controls life. There are, therefore, no prayers, for there is no god or goddess to whom to pray. Later, Buddha himself came to be thought of as a god, but this was contrary to his own ideas.

Like Jesus, Buddha did not write down his teachings. After his death, his disciples, in council, compiled his philosophy into books called *Sutras*.

Although Buddhism was for a time strong in India, its hold upon the people gradually grew weaker and weaker until less than 1 percent of Indians today call themselves Buddhists. The teachings of the "Enlightened One," however, have influenced many Hindus, who accepted them and added them to their own religion. Thus, many of the beliefs of Buddhism have been absorbed by the tolerant Hinduism.

Sikhs. The Sikhs (SEEKS) are followers of a religion founded in the 15th century by Nanak (NAH-nak), a Hindu religious teacher. He was called *Guru* ("Great Teacher"). Nanak sought to reconcile Hindus and Muslims who lived side by side with differing religious and social ideas. His new religion drew its ideas from both Hinduism and Islam.

An elderly Sikh stands near the end of the causeway that leads to the Golden Temple in Amritsar. The Golden Temple, in the background, is the holiest site of the Sikh religion.

The Sikhs believe in one God, not in many as in the Hindu religion. They do not believe in the Hindu caste system, but do believe in reincarnation. They have their own language, Punjabi, which also is spoken by many Muslims in Pakistan. Their sacred book, *Granth Sahib* (grahnt sah-EEB), contains hymns, rituals, and stories about moral conduct. Sikhs do not cut their hair, and Sikh men usually wear it in a **turban**, a long piece of cloth wrapped around the head. Sikhs do not use tobacco or alcohol. The men always wear an iron bracelet and a two-edged dagger. Their names always include the word *Singh,* which means "lion."

Most of the 14 million Sikhs live in the Punjab, but they are also found in many of the larger cities of India. The Sikhs are excellent warriors. Their military history goes back hundreds of years, when they first opposed the Islamic rulers in northern India. Later they served in the British army, and today they are among the best soldiers in the Indian army.

Christianity. The earliest Christian communities were established, according to tradition, by the Apostle Thomas, who is believed to have preached in India soon after Jesus died. Syrian Christians in the 5th century, Jesuit missionaries in the 16th century, and Protestant missionaries from the 17th century on also established churches and converted Indians to their faith. Many of the 18 million Christian Indians live in southern India today.

Parsis. The Parsis (PAHR-seez) are Zoroastrians (zoh-roh-AS-tree-uhnz), followers of a religion founded in Persia by Zoroaster (zoh-roh-AS-tuhr) around 1000 B.C. Ahura-Mazda (AH-hoo-ruh MAZ-duh) is their God, and Zoroaster is his prophet. Parsis are descended from refugees who fled the Islamic conquest of Persia (modern Iran) in the 7th and 8th centuries. They live mostly around Bombay.

The Parsis venerate fire as a symbol of purity. They bathe before praying morning and night. They do not believe in missionary work, and only a descendant of a Parsi may be a Parsi. Zoroaster taught that one's good deeds during life determine one's life after death, so Parsis are noted for their benevolence. They do not bury their dead. When a person dies, his or her body is placed on the top of a Tower of Silence to be picked clean by vultures.

The Parsis were not bound by the dietary and caste restrictions of the Hindus, so they adapted easily to the Western ideas brought into India by the British. Although there are only about 150,000 Parsis today, they have become successful leaders in industry, commerce, and the professions. The great iron and steel plants of the Parsi Tata family are examples of the accomplishments of well-educated, hard-working Parsi business people.

REVIEWING THE CHAPTER

I. Building Your Vocabulary

In your notebook, write the correct term that matches the definition.

dharma	caste	*Ramayana*
Jainism	reincarnation	Sikhs

1. Hindu belief that upon death, a person's soul moves into the body of another living thing

2. followers of a religion that combines elements of Hinduism and Islam

3. set of rules that Hindus believe each living thing must follow to be promoted in its next reincarnation

4. Hindu epic that tells the story of the god Rama and his wife Sita

5. religion of India whose followers practice nonviolence to all living things

6. one of the hereditary classes that divide Hindu society

II. Understanding the Facts

In your notebook, write the numbers from 1 to 5. Write the letter of the correct answer to each question next to its number.

1. How many gods and goddesses do devout Hindus worship?
   a. one   b. many   c. none

2. Which is the highest class in the Indian caste system?
   a. military   b. priests   c. workers

3. Who are Vishnu and Siva?
   a. deities in the Hindu religion
   b. leaders of the Islamic religion
   c. rulers of territories in central India

4. What are the *Vedas*?
   a. the invaders of north India
   b. the rulers of central India
   c. sacred hymns and prayers of the Hindu religion
5. Which animal do Hindus hold sacred?
   a. the camel   b. the cow   c. the elephant

III. Thinking It Through

In your notebook, write the numbers from 1 to 5. Write the letter of the correct conclusion to each sentence next to its number.

1. The basic ideas of Hinduism were
   a. taught by Muhammad during the 7th century A.D.
   b. started in Magadha by a teacher known as Mahavira.
   c. developed in the Indus Valley civilization and by the Aryan invaders of 1500 B.C.
   d. taught by a prince named Siddhartha Gautama.
2. Hinduism has made it difficult for other religions to gain a foothold in India because
   a. Hinduism is the official state religion of all India.
   b. almost all Indians practice Hinduism.
   c. Hindus classify all those of other religions as Untouchables, or among the lowest class.
   d. Hinduism is tolerant of other religions and willing to add new beliefs to its ancient ones.
3. Hinduism and Islam share the following belief:
   a. There is only one God.
   b. It is not proper to make images of living things.
   c. A pilgrimage is an important part of one's religion.
   d. It is not proper to eat meat.
4. The caste system is reinforced by the Hindu concept of
   a. Mahabharata.   b. reincarnation.
   c. nirvana.   d. submission to God.
5. When the caste system was strictly followed, a person's best hope for rising in rank was by
   a. marrying into a family of a higher caste.
   b. earning enough money to acquire a higher caste.
   c. achieving a higher caste in the next reincarnation.
   d. obtaining higher caste as a reward for military service.

DEVELOPING CRITICAL THINKING SKILLS

1. How are the ideas of *dharma, karma,* and reincarnation related?
2. What social forces maintain the caste system?
3. Why is it difficult to characterize Hinduism?
4. Compare the teachings of Hinduism and Buddhism about the way a person can achieve true happiness.

INTERPRETING GRAPHS

The circle graphs show the percentages of the total populations of India, Pakistan, and Bangladesh that practice various religions. Use the graphs to answer the following questions.

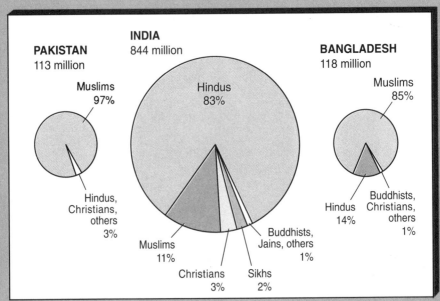

Religions of the Indian Subcontinent

Source: Universal Almanac, 1992

1. Compare the percentage of Hindus in India to the percentage of Muslims in Bangladesh. Which country has the higher percentage of its main religion?

2. Which country has the highest percentage of Christians?

3. Which country has the least amount of religious diversity?

4. What additional information would you need to decide whether there were more Buddhists in India than in Bangladesh?

5. Draw circle graphs to illustrate the following information: 99.5% of the world's Hindus live in southern Asia; 0.2% live in Africa. Of the world's Muslims, 26.4% live in Africa; 65.5% live in south Asia; 3.9% live in the republics of the Commonwealth of Independent States; and 2.7% live in east Asia.

ENRICHMENT AND EXPLORATION

1. Working with a group, make a list of questions about Hinduism and Buddhism. Classify your group's questions under the following headings: basic beliefs, dietary laws, rituals and festivals, leaders. Divide the topics among the members of the group. Each member should do research on one of the topics, trying to find the answers to each of the questions. When the research is completed, each group member should present the report to the group and, after revision according to suggestions from the group, to the whole class.

2. Prepare a dramatic reading of a short portion of the *Ramayana*, and present the reading to the class. The section in Book 1 about the breaking of the bow is a good dramatic selection.

3. Do research on yoga. Write a short report on the various forms of yoga, including its origins in Indian philosophy and the types of yoga popular in the United States. Learn one or two very simple yoga positions and include their descriptions in your report.

4. Do research on the *mudras*, or hand gestures, used in sculptures of the Buddha. Explain the *mudra* in several statues of Buddha.

5. Make a replica in clay or a drawing of a statue of Siva or Vishnu. Prepare a description of the qualities of the deity that are illustrated.

INDIA AND THE WORLD

c. 2500 B.C.–A.D. 1858

c. 3100–332 B.C.	*Ancient Egyptian civilization*
c. 2500–1500 B.C.	Indus civilization flourishes.
c. 1500 B.C.	Aryans invade India.
563 B.C.	Birth of Siddhartha Gautama, the Buddha
c. 518 B.C.	Persians invade northwestern India.
480 B.C.	*Golden Age begins in Greece.*
326 B.C.	Alexander the Great invades India.
332 B.C.	Chandragupta founds Maurya Empire.
273–232 B.C.	Reign of Asoka
c. A.D. 30	*Beginning of Christianity*
c. A.D. 300	Gupta Empire is established.
c. A.D. 500	Huns invade India.
A.D. 606–647	Reign of Harsha, last of the great Gupta kings
A.D. 632	*Muhammad dies.*
A.D. 711	Muslims conquer present-day Pakistan.
A.D. 800–1100	*African kingdom of Ghana*
1206–1398	Sultanate of Delhi
1492	*Columbus lands at San Salvador.*
1525	Babur invades India.
1556–1605	Mogul Empire is at its height under Akbar.
1628–1658	Reign of Shah Jehan
1776	*U.S. Declaration of Independence*
1858	British depose last Mogul emperor.

3 Early Civilizations and Great Empires

India has a long and continuous culture. It is possibly 5,000 years old, almost as old as the ancient Egyptian and Mesopotamian cultures. However, unlike the latter, which disappeared under the impact of foreign invaders, the culture of India never lost its identity, even though often attacked. Rather, it added some of the invaders' beliefs and customs to its own and thus enriched its own practices and traditions.

India's long history before independence (1947) can, for the sake of convenience, be divided into four periods:

- The Indus Valley period (c. 3000–c. 1500 B.C.)
- The Hindu period (c. 1500 B.C.–c. A.D. 1200)
- The Islamic period (c. 1200–1760)
- The British period (1760–1947)

The British period will be the subject of Chapter 4. This chapter examines the first three of these periods.

THE INDUS VALLEY PERIOD (c. 3000 B.C.–c. 1500 B.C.)

About 3000 B.C., civilization, in the sense of an organized system of government and developed settlements of people, grew up almost at the same time in the valleys of the Nile, Tigris and Euphrates, and Indus rivers. Much is known about the civilizations of Egypt and Mesopotamia, for their people left many records that scholars can read. The writing of the Indus people, on the other hand, has not yet been deciphered, so that knowledge of this Indus culture is incomplete. Enough has been discovered in the last 70 years, however, to reveal a civilization that compares favorably with other ancient civilizations.

Harappa and Mohenjo-Daro. In the early 1920s British and Indian archaeologists uncovered a city buried on the banks of the Indus River. Further excavations uncovered other towns stretching over a distance of 1,000 miles. The two most important cities were Harappa (huh-RAP-uh), on the left bank of the Ravi River, a tributary of the Indus, and Mohenjo-Daro (moh-HEN-joh DAHR-oh), on the right bank of the Indus some 250 miles from its mouth. It is believed that the towns and cities may have had a central government, because such things as weights and measures, the layout of city streets, and the bricks used in buildings are similar.

No one knows where these people came from or how long they lived in the Indus valley. Research reveals that for at least 1,000 years these inhabitants enjoyed comfortable living. They carried on extensive trading not only among themselves but also with the peoples of Mesopotamia. Indus seals, emblems, and other objects have been found in Mesopotamia dating prior to 2000 B.C.

The towns and cities that have been discovered tell a great deal about the people who lived in them. The towns were carefully planned, with main streets that were 30 feet (9 meters) wide. Each city had an efficient sewage system and public baths. The houses were made of solidly baked bricks that have not crumbled over the centuries. Many of the houses were two stories high and had bathrooms.

Most of the people were farmers who raised wheat, barley, and peas. Cotton was also grown and woven into cloth and sold to countries

A scene in the ruins of Harappa, one of the principal cities of the Indus Valley civilization. The large circular structure is a well. Reconstructed irrigation channels can be seen leading away from the well and past the remains of buildings.

far away. It is probable that cotton cloth was first woven by the people in the Indus valley. Animals were domesticated, so that water buffalo and other animals were put to work. To **domesticate** animals is to tame them and breed them for human use. Skilled crafts workers made pottery, bracelets, figurines, and other objects from copper, bronze, gold, and silver.

The Aryan Invasions. The Indus Valley civilization came to an end around 1500 B.C. Some scientists believe that the end had natural causes, such as earthquakes, the rivers' changing course, or exhaustion of the farmland. Others think it fell to the Aryans, invaders from the great steppe (plains) land stretching from Poland to Central Asia. Whether they conquered the Indus civilization or arrived after its collapse, there is no question that the Aryans arrived. They were a tall, fair people, who spoke a language related to those of the Greeks, Romans, Celts, Germans, and Slavs.

The Aryan invasion of India was not a single action. It took place over hundreds of years and involved many groups. The Aryans made servants of the people they conquered, or they drove them out of their homes into other parts of India. It is believed that the Dravidian-speaking peoples of southern India are descended from these people who fled the invaders.

THE HINDU PERIOD (1500 B.C.–A.D. 1200)

The Aryans gradually overcame and intermarried with the inhabitants of the Indus valley. They also moved eastward across the Punjab and into the Ganges valley, driving out the people and then settling in villages to farm and raise their flocks.

Early Aryan Culture, 1500–1000 B.C. Much that is known about the early Aryan invaders of the Indus valley comes from the *Rig-Vedas*, a collection of religious literature. These hymns paint a picture of a war-loving people who fought from horse-drawn chariots. They used a language that later became Sanskrit. They loved dancing and music and were fond of gambling, particularly with dice. They worshiped many gods and goddesses of nature. Wealth was reckoned in flocks of cattle and sheep. The chief of each tribe was a *rajah* (RAH-juh); the word is related to Latin *rex*, meaning "king."

During this period, the Aryans extended their control into the Ganges River valley, northward to the Himalaya Mountains, and southward to the Mahanadi River. The great epics of Indian literature, the *Ramayana* and the *Mahabharata*, are the chief sources of information about this period.

By the 6th century B.C. a society very different from the original Aryan emerged from a fusion of Aryan and Dravidian cultures. The *Upanishads* represent this new society. Great gods and goddesses like Vishnu, Siva, and Devi were worshiped. The concepts of rebirth, of fate (*karma*), and of duty (*dharma*) had taken form. The cow was worshiped as a sacred animal. Hinduism was changing into its present form.

There were also great changes socially and politically. The caste system took shape. What were once tribal settlements became small kingdoms. Cities began to grow. New trades and crafts developed, such as jewelry-making, metalworking, basketry, weaving, carpentry, and pottery-making. Many crops, including rice, were raised. The kings grew in power, and the influence of new religious leaders challenged the Brahmans, the Hindu priestly caste. Continual fighting between rival kings prevented the creation of a united country during these centuries. Frequent contacts between the kings and the Brahman priestly class contributed to the development of new religious ideas.

During the 6th century B.C. two new religions arose in north India. One was Jainism, founded by Mahavira (540–467 B.C.). Its central idea was *ahimsa*, or nonviolence (see page 45). The other religion, established by Siddhartha Gautama (563–483 B.C.), was Buddhism (see pages 45–47). With Buddhism came opposition to the caste system, and stress on the elimination of all desire as the condition necessary to escape from the burden of successive rebirths. Both of these religious movements influenced the dominant Hindu religion.

Persian and Greek Contacts.   Darius I (dah-REYE-uhs), King of Persia, invaded northwest India about 518 B.C. He conquered the Indus valley and West Punjab regions and added them to his already large empire, which stretched westward as far as Greece and Egypt. Trade and commerce developed between India and Persia. Some Indian soldiers fought with the Persian emperor Xerxes (ZURK-seez) when he invaded Greece in 479 B.C. Persian control over its Indian states weakened, however, and small independent Indian kingdoms were established.

Then in 326 B.C. Alexander the Great, who had conquered the Persian Empire, crossed into northwest India through one of the passes in the mountains. He helped one of the Indian kings defeat several rival rulers. However, Alexander's weary Greek troops refused to go farther with him and threatened to mutiny. Alexander gave in to his soldiers' demands to return home, loaded them into boats, and sailed down the Indus River into the Arabian Sea.

Chandragupta and the Maurya Empire. In the power vacuum left after Alexander's departure, one of the small kingdoms in northeastern India emerged to become the seat of a large empire. Chandragupta Maurya (chuhn-drah-GOOP-tah MAH-oor-yah) seized control of the throne of the kings of Magadha (MUHG-uhd-uh) in 332 B.C. and, before his death in 297 B.C., he had conquered rival kings to the north and west of his own kingdom. He established firm rule over territory that stretched into what is now Afghanistan in the west and to the Ganges River in the east.

The Maurya Empire was highly **centralized**, that is, controlled by one central government rather than by local governments. It also was powerful, with secret police to maintain order and a large standing army of 700,000 soldiers and 9,000 elephants. Chandragupta's son, Bindusara (bin-doo-SAH-rah), who ruled until 273 B.C., added to the empire by conquering much of the Deccan. Bindusara's son, Asoka (ah-SOH-kah), added eastern India to the realm. For more than 40 years (273–232 B.C.), Asoka ruled an empire that included much of the Indian subcontinent.

The Reign of Asoka. Asoka was one of the greatest rulers in history. He spent the first few of the 40 years he ruled fighting and enlarging his empire. The more than 100,000 deaths that resulted from his conquest in 261 B.C. of Kalinga, on the east coast, horrified him. He gave up war and spent the rest of his life following the path of nonviolence and peace. He even gave up the sport of hunting, the traditional pastime of kings. He became a Buddhist and tried to win the obedience of his subjects by kindness.

He built hospitals and rest houses throughout his empire. He had wells dug every mile beside the roads for the benefit of travelers and animals. To inspire the people, he had messages of tolerance and kindness inscribed on rocks and in caves throughout the empire.

Asoka sent teachers to all parts of his empire to spread education, and brought many students to the universities that were established in various parts of the realm. He sent missionaries to other countries. His brother helped convert the king of Ceylon (present-day Sri Lanka) to

CASE STUDY:
Mauryan Government

The following selection is part of some principles of government suggested by Kautilya, minister to Chandragupta, the first of the Mauryan dynasty.

Only if a king is himself energetically active, do his officers follow him energetically. If he is sluggish, they too remain sluggish. And, besides, they eat up his works. He is thereby easily overpowered by his enemies. Therefore, he should ever dedicate himself energetically to activity.

He should divide the day as well as the night into eight parts. . . . During the first one-eighth part of the day, he should listen to reports pertaining to the organization of law and order and to income and expenditure. During the second, he should attend to the affairs of the urban and the rural population. During the third, he should take his bath and meal and devote himself to study. During the fourth, he should receive gold and the departmental heads. During the fifth, he should hold consultations with the council of ministers through correspondence and also keep himself informed of the secret reports brought by spies. During the sixth, he should devote himself freely to amusement or listen to the counsel of the ministers. During the seventh, he should inspect the military formations of elephants, cavalry, chariots, and infantry. During the eighth, he, together with the commander-in-chief of the army, should make plans for campaigns of conquest. When the day has come to an end he should offer the evening prayers.

William Theodore de Bary, *Sources of Indian Tradition.* New York: Columbia University Press, 1958, pages 246–248.

1. Do you consider these suggestions practical? Would they work for a head of state today? Explain.
2. What can modern historians infer from this selection about Chandragupta and the Maurya dynasty?

The capital, or top section, of a pillar erected by Asoka at Sarnath. There are four lions altogether, one facing in each direction. The wheel below the lions is now the central symbol on India's flag.

Buddhism. His daughter established a convent there. Teachers were sent to Egypt, to North Africa, and to Greece.

The Maurya Empire after Asoka.   Asoka's empire gradually fell apart after his death. His descendants were not strong rulers. Rivals challenged their power, and invaders from outside the subcontinent added to the breakdown of central authority. The first invaders were Greeks who, in the 2nd century B.C., created a kingdom that included Afghanistan and the Punjab in northwest India. A century later, Scythians (SITH-ee-uhnz), nomads from central Asia, established their brief rule over all of western India as far south as the Deccan. Still later, during the 2nd century A.D., Kushans (koo-SHAHNZ), another central Asian people, conquered the Scythians and native Indians and created a large kingdom in north India.

Kingdoms of South India.   During these centuries of continual warfare, and of the rise and fall of small and large kingdoms in northern and central India, the southern part of India was having a similar history. Rulers of small kingdoms continually fought each other for power and influence. The southern part of India was not invaded by peoples from the north, however, because of the tangle of forest and hill country that separated the Deccan from the upper parts of the Jumna River.

61

The southern part of the subcontinent was the home of the Dravidian peoples. Over the centuries they gradually divided into separate kingdoms, each with its own language. Some of the cities on the coasts of south India engaged in trade with the West, with northern India, and with the East Indies. Fine textiles, pepper, drugs, woods, ivory, and precious stones were exchanged for gold and silver.

The Gupta Dynasty. In the 4th century A.D., the Gupta (GOOP-tah) dynasty (ruling house) arose in the north. It centered around Magadha, the old capital of the Mauryas. The first ruler, Chandragupta I, was famous as a conqueror, musician, and poet. His grandson, Chandragupta II, reigned for over 40 years, and added Bengal, the upper Jumna–Ganges valley, and parts of central India to his empire. The next ruler conquered the northwestern provinces of India almost to the Indus River. The last of the great Gupta kings was Harsha (A.D. 606–647), who unified northern India.

These two and a half centuries are known as the "Golden Age" of ancient Indian history. A good deal is known about India of this period from the wealth of Sanskrit literature. In addition, many of its temples and sculptures still exist, and many coins and inscriptions have been discovered. Two Chinese Buddhist pilgrims left records of the prosperity and good government of the empire. Fa-Hsien (FAH shee-EN) spent ten years traveling around during the reign of Chandragupta II, and Hsüan-Tsang (shee-AHN DZAHNG) spent eight years in Harsha's empire.

Art, science, and literature flourished during the Gupta period. Sanskrit had become the official and literary language. The poet and playwright Kalidasa (KAH-lee-DAH-sah) wrote his masterpiece *Sakuntala* (sah-koon-TAH-lah) in the 5th century. It is the story of a king's love for a hermit's daughter, their marriage, separation, and reunion. Kalidasa's beautiful poem "The Cloud Messenger" tells of a lonely husband far from home who sends a cloud with a message of love to his wife. Kalidasa is sometimes called the "Indian Shakespeare" because those who can read both Sanskrit and English see the two poets as equals.

Indian mathematicians were the first to develop the concept of zero, and they worked out a decimal system. The so-called Arabic numerals were developed in India and were learned by Arab traders, who carried the system to Europe. The value of pi [π] was determined to be 3.1416. Doctors performed plastic surgery operations, indicating a good knowledge of medicine. Great universities with free board and tuition were provided for talented students.

*The sculpture-filled interior of one of the Ajanta Caves,
in the state of Maharashtra northeast of Bombay.*

While many of the buildings of the Gupta period have disappeared,
a few beautiful ones remain. There also are Buddhist paintings and
sculpture in the caves at Ajanta (uh-JUHNT-uh) in central India and at
Sigiriya (sih-GIHR-yuh) in Sri Lanka. In the practical arts, the Indians
were far advanced. The Iron Pillar near Delhi stands 23 feet high, is 16
inches in diameter, and weighs almost six tons. It was erected about
A.D. 400 to commemorate one of Chandragupta's victories and has not
yet rusted.

During the Gupta rule travel and trade flourished between India,
southern Europe, and China. Indian ambassadors represented their
ruler at the Roman court. Indian and Chinese scholars exchanged visits.
The influence of Indian culture on Chinese ways of thought, religion,
and everyday life was considerable.

The Downfall of the Guptas.   Invading Huns from Central Asia (c. A.D. 500), followed by other Central Asian, Turkish, and Mongolian invaders, brought about the end of the Gupta dynasty. By the end of the 7th century, there was political confusion in northern India, a condition that lasted for 500 years.

During this period of trouble, there was no unity. Small kingdoms were established, fought each other, and died out. Some of the northwestern states, notably those of the Rajput kings, gained considerable fame for their valiant but vain efforts to keep out the new invaders, the Muslims.

India in the 12th Century.   These were the conditions that the Muslims met in India:

- Boundaries of the many kingdoms were constantly changing.

- The rulers were regarded as divine-right kings, with absolute powers to protect the land from invasion and promote the "right way" of life as set forth in the sacred texts of Hinduism.

- The government in many kingdoms owned the mines, the forests, and the spinning and weaving establishments, and it was responsible for the construction and maintenance of irrigation works so necessary for the farmers.

- Hinduism was the main religion of the people, although Buddhism had won many converts during and after the reign of Asoka in the 3rd century B.C. The religious tolerance practiced by many Hindu rulers permitted the spread of Buddhism, but it gradually died out in India, particularly after the 8th century A.D.

- The influence of Sanskrit culture and caste organization provided religious and cultural unity for Indians.

- Village life was the basis of the Indian economy and way of living. A hereditary head man, usually a wealthy peasant, was in charge.

- From one-quarter to one-third of the crops raised were paid in taxes.

THE ISLAMIC PERIOD (A.D. 1200–1760)

In the 7th century A.D. a new religion arose in what is today Saudi Arabia. This religion, called Islam, was founded by Muhammad. Within a short time after his death in A.D. 632, his followers captured Jerusalem and Damascus and conquered all of Palestine, Syria, and Egypt. Within a century, Islamic armies had spread westward across North Africa into Spain and France, where they were finally stopped at the Battle of Tours in A.D. 732. In the same century, other armies pushed eastward to Baghdad and into central Asia. In A.D. 711, a young Arabian general named Muhammad ibn Kasim fought his way up the Indus valley, in what is now Pakistan, and conquered the territory. It marked the beginning of Islamic conquests in India.

For the next 300 years, the chief relations between India and the Islamic rulers at their capital, Baghdad, were through trade. Personal contacts between Hindus and Muslims in ports along the southwest coast of India became more common during these years, and many Hindus were converted to Islam.

About A.D. 1000 a Turkish chief named Mahmud of Ghazni raided northern India for more than 20 years, sacking cities, destroying Hindu temples and statues of the gods and goddesses, and carrying away treasures, particularly jewels. A century and a half later, in 1139, another invader, the Persian Muhammad Ghori, conquered Delhi and other important cities in northern India. He established an independent Islamic state, called the Sultanate of Delhi after its capital city. It lasted until 1526.

Growth of Islam in India. The Muslims of India, beginning as traders on the southwestern coast, became in the course of time one-fourth of the entire population. How did this growth take place?

Many conquered Hindus converted to the Islamic faith. Since government services were open only to Muslims, it was worthwhile for an ambitious person to convert. For others it was a way to escape taxes levied on non-Muslims.

Entire lower castes in some areas went over to Islam. This occurred in Bengal, where caste discrimination was severe. It helps to explain why Bengali Muslims fought to establish their independence from India, first as part of Pakistan and later as the independent nation of Bangladesh.

Rise of the Mogul Empire. In the 13th and 14th centuries, armies of the Sultanate of Delhi conquered parts of central and southern India and controlled an area larger than had ever been united before. However, in the same years the sultanate was fiercely attacked by Mongols from northern and central Asia. Under Genghis Khan, in the

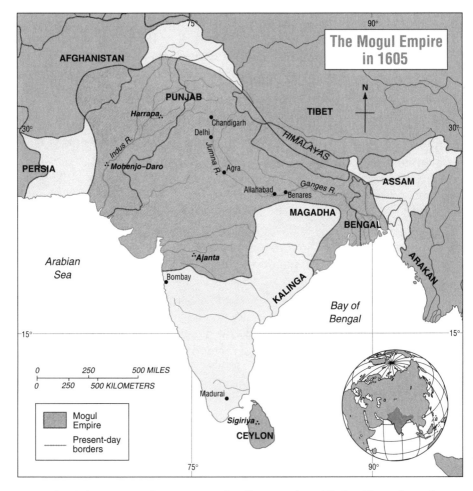

The Mogul Empire in 1605

AFGHANISTAN

PUNJAB

Harrapa

Chandigarh

Delhi

Indus R.

Jumna R.

PERSIA

Mohenjo-Daro

Agra

Allahabad

Benares

Ganges R.

HIMALAYAS

TIBET

ASSAM

MAGADHA

BENGAL

ARAKAN

Arabian
Sea

Ajanta

Bombay

KALINGA

Bay of
Bengal

0   250   500 MILES
0   250   500 KILOMETERS

Madurai

Mogul
Empire

Present-day
borders

Sigiriya

CEYLON

early 13th century, they overran the Ganges plain. Under Tamerlane, in 1398, they marched into northern India and sacked Delhi.

In 1525 the Mongols returned once again, and this time they stayed. Babur (BAH-buhr), a direct descendant of Genghis Khan and Tamerlane, invaded India. Before his death in 1530, Babur had conquered a large part of northern India. Babur, who was a Muslim, founded a new Islamic dynasty in India, the **Mogul** dynasty.

Babur's grandson, Akbar (AHK-bahr), created and supervised a strong administration. In time he controlled much of east, west, and central India. Akbar looked for the most capable people, offering high salaries. He reformed the system of tax collecting.

Akbar practiced religious toleration. He repealed the tax levied on Hindus and opened the public service to them. He himself married two

Hindu princesses. Akbar encouraged learning and education throughout his kingdom.

Mogul Culture. Under the successors of Akbar, Mogul culture flourished. Great mosques, tombs, and palaces were built, and exquisite gardens were laid out. Paintings of luxurious court life and of nature studies are excellent examples of Mogul art.

Architecture reached its peak during the 30-year reign (1628–1658) of Akbar's grandson, Shah Jahan (SHAH jah-HAHN). He is best known

The hand-painted book illustration, left, is an example of Mogul art from the late 1500s, during the reign of Akbar. It shows Alexander the Great, who had invaded India in 326 B.C., being lowered into the waters of the Indus in a glass jar. The magnificent building below is the legendary Taj Mahal, built in the city of Agra by Akbar's grandson, Shah Jahan, as his wife's tomb.

to the West as the ruler who built the Taj Mahal (TAZH muh-HAHL) at Agra as a tomb for his wife. The beauty of the Taj Mahal is in the lovely curves of its marble dome and in the designs and religious inscriptions, done with costly semi-precious stones, that decorate its walls. It is said to have taken 20,000 workers more than 15 years to build the memorial. In addition to the Taj Mahal, Shah Jahan was also responsible for the building of the Red Fort in old Delhi, including its palaces, audience halls, baths, gardens, and magnificent Peacock Throne.

The riches of the shah were beyond anything known in Europe at that time. Silks from China and rugs from Persia were found on his palace's walls and floors. Gold and silver vases were everywhere. The Peacock Throne on which the shah sat was inlaid with costly jewels. It has been estimated that the value of Shah Jahan's treasure was worth in present values between $3 and $4 billion.

Downfall of the Moguls.   The peace and harmony that Akbar had so carefully fostered eventually ended. Shah Jehan's son Aurangzeb (OHR-rung-zeb), who reigned from 1659 to 1707, destroyed many Hindu temples, earning the hatred of the Hindu princes and the Hindu population by his intolerance. He also angered the Sikhs by executing their leader. They became violently anti-Muslim, established a kingdom in the Punjab in northern India, and successfully defied Islamic efforts to conquer them.

Another group that rebelled against Mogul intolerance was the Marathas (muh-RAH-tuhz), who lived in the Western Ghat Mountains on the southwest coast near Bombay. The Marathas successfully waged guerrilla warfare against Mogul armies sent out to destroy them. Under their leader Sivaji (SIH-vah-jee), the Marathas established a strong state in central and western India.

After Aurangzeb's death in 1707, the Mogul empire quickly fell to pieces. One province after another broke away and established independence. The Nadir Shah (NAH-dihr SHAH) of Persia invaded Mogul territory, defeated its army, and carried off the crown jewels and the famous Peacock Throne to Persia. Civil war further weakened the empire.

In 1803, Shah Alam II came under British control. For 50 years his successors kept their title until finally, in 1858, the British sent the last Mogul emperor into exile in Burma (now Myanmar).

The Mogul dynasty was the last independent Indian dynasty. Control of India passed to a people from a small island far away in the Atlantic Ocean, the British.

Chapter 3
CHECKUP

REVIEWING THE CHAPTER

I. Building Your Vocabulary

In your notebook, write the correct term that matches the definition.

Gupta	Taj Mahal	Asoka
Maurya	Mogul	Kalidasa

1. Mauryan emperor who added eastern India to the realm and ruled the empire at its height

2. one of the Mongol descendants who ruled a great empire in India from 1525 until 1858

3. dynasty that extended across northern India in the 4th century A.D.

4. early Indian empire founded in northeastern India by Chandragupta Maurya in 332 B.C.

5. tomb built at Agra by the Mogul Shah Jahan for his wife

6. dramatist of the Gupta period

II. Understanding the Facts

In your notebook, write the numbers from 1 to 5. Write the letter of the correct answer to each question next to its number.

1. On which river did the earliest Indian civilization flourish?
   a. Ganges   b. Indus   c. Brahmaputra

2. What does the Indian word *raja* mean?
   a. god   b. ruler   c. peasant

3. Which period was India's "Golden Age"?
   a. rule of the Gupta kings   b. conquests of the Maurya rulers
   c. rule of Mogul dynasty

4. Members of which castes converted to Islam in large numbers in Bengal?
   a. lower   b. upper   c. middle

5. Forces of what nation ended the Mogul dynasty?
   a. the French   b. the British   c. the Chinese

III. Thinking It Through

In your notebook, write the numbers from 1 to 5. Write the letter of the correct conclusion to each sentence next to its number.

1. The culture of India differs from the cultures of ancient Egypt and Mesopotamia in that:
   a. India was never invaded by outsiders.
   b. India was repeatedly invaded by outsiders, while Egypt and Mesopotamia were not influenced by foreigners.
   c. the Indian culture retained its own practices and identity despite repeated invasions by outsiders.
   d. the culture of India is not nearly so old.

2. Each of the following statements about the early Aryan culture is correct *except*:
   a. Aryans used horses and raised cattle and sheep.
   b. Aryans worshiped many gods and goddesses.
   c. Aryans made servants of the people they conquered or forced them to move into other parts of India.
   d. Aryans had no written language.

3. Alexander the Great:
   a. was prevented by his soldiers from attempting to extend his empire into India.
   b. took over the Indian territory conquered by Darius I of Persia.
   c. was killed by trying to invade India.
   d. became the founder of one India's great religions.

4. The Indian emperor who practiced nonviolence, founded schools and hospitals, and had messages of tolerance carved on rocks and in caves was named:
   a. Chandragupta Maurya.   b. Asoka.
   c. Shah Jahan.   d. Akbar.

5. The Mogul Empire began to dissolve when:
   a. the Delhi Sultanate took advantage of internal feuding in the empire to break off several kingdoms.
   b. the British destroyed the empire in several great battles.
   c. Mogul intolerance angered Hindus, Sikhs, and Marathas.
   d. the great Hindu leader Chandragupta led a combined force of Hindus and Muslims against the Moguls.

DEVELOPING CRITICAL THINKING SKILLS

1. What are some questions that might be answered if scholars could decipher the writing of the Indus culture?
2. Using the findings of archaeologists at Harappa and Mohenjo-Daro as a base, make some speculations about the values and goals of the people who lived there.
3. Speculate on what might have happened if Alexander's soldiers had followed him into India.
4. Compare the Gupta and Mogul empires in terms of the size of the empires, cultural achievements, and the end of the dynasties.

READING A TIME BOX

Use the Time Box on page 54 to find answers to the following questions. Write the answers in your notebook.

1. Which great Indian empire established its rule before the Huns invaded India?
2. In what year did Babur found the Mongul empire?
3. Which of the following events occurred second?
   a. the birth of the Buddha
   b. the founding of the Maurya empire
   c. the reign of Shah Jahan
   d. the Aryan invasion of India

ENRICHMENT AND EXPLORATION

1. Using an encyclopedia, prepare a short biography of one of the following: Asoka, Shah Jahan, Kalidasa.
2. Using an encyclopedia, indicate the boundaries of the Maurya Empire, the Gupta Empire, and the Mogul Empire on an outline map of India. Give your map a title and make a key.
3. Read more about one of the following topics and prepare a short report: the varieties of Indian architecture, Indian gardens, paintings of the Mogul period.

71

INDIA AND THE WORLD
1492–1876

1492	*Columbus lands at San Salvador.*
1498	Vasco da Gama finds sea route to India.
1509–1515	Portugal establishes trading posts in India.
1612	British East India Company establishes its first trading post.
1664	French East India Company is established.
1757	British defeat French at Plassey.
1757–1766	Clive governs Bengal.
1772–1785	Warren Hastings governs holdings of British East India Company.
1776	*U.S. Declaration of Independence*
1786–1793	Governorship of Lord Cornwallis
1789	*French Revolution begins.*
1789–1805	East India Company becomes strongest power in India.
1813	Parliament ends East India Company's monopoly.
1828–1835	Lord Bentinck introduces western reforms.
1833	East India Company becomes political agent of the British government.
1848–1856	British conquest of India is completed.
1853	Competitive exams are introduced for entry to Indian Civil Service.
1854	Departments of Public Instruction established throughout India.
1857	Great Indian (or Sepoy) Mutiny
1858	British government takes over holding of the British East India Company.
1861–1865	*U.S. Civil War*
1876	Queen Victoria takes title "Empress of India."

4 The British In India

During the nearly 100 years from 1760 to 1858, the rule of India was gradually taken over by Great Britain. The British, however, were not the first Europeans to arrive in India.

EUROPEAN INTEREST IN INDIA

European interest in the products of India went back many hundreds of years. Spices from Asia, tea, jewels, and fabrics of silk and cotton had been known in European countries for a long time. Indian products were used in the West 2,000 years ago during the days of the Roman Empire.

The Spice Trade. The Indians on the Malabar coast produced pepper. Other spices were brought by sea to South India from the East Indies. From India these spices were shipped, mostly by land, through Egypt, Iraq, and the Turkish lands to trading centers at Constantinople and Alexandria. From there, Italian merchants from Venice, Genoa, and Pisa took them to Europe. At every place along the way, tolls and bribes had to be paid before these goods were allowed to move on. As a result, the prices of spices were high by the time they reached Europe. There, in spite of the high prices, they were in great demand.

Why did Europeans want these spices so badly that they were willing to pay large sums for them? One reason was their importance in preserving meats. Because there was no winter food for cows and pigs, many animals had to be killed in the late fall. However, there was no known way, except with spices, to keep the meat from spoiling. Spices were also valuable in flavoring the sour wine that was cultivated in many parts of Europe.

The Turkish capture of Constantinople in 1453 made it difficult for the Italian traders to continue their business. The Turks placed high taxes on goods coming in and going out of the city. Since the overland trade routes that had been built up over the centuries were blocked, European countries on the Atlantic coast began to look for new ways to get to India and the Far East.

Arrival of the First Europeans. The first Europeans to arrive in India and set up permanent settlements were also the last to leave. These were the Portuguese. Portuguese sea captains explored the west coast of Africa looking for a water route to the Indies. After a voyage of nearly 11 months, Vasco da Gama sailed around the Cape of Good Hope and dropped anchor in May 1498 at Calicut, on the southwestern coast of India. This marked the beginning of European trade in India, and led eventually to control of the entire subcontinent by foreigners.

Vasco da Gama was followed by others. The wealth of the Indian trade prompted Portugal to send more ships, soldiers, and administrators to India to establish trading posts. Alfonso de Albuquerque (ahl-boo-KAIR-kuh), between 1509 and 1515 took control of various port areas and the cities of Goa (GOH-uh), Damão (duh-MOWN), and Diu (DEE-oo), and increased trade between the East Indies and Portugal.

During the 16th century, the Portuguese had a **monopoly** on the trade between India and Europe. A monopoly is exclusive ownership or control of something. Portuguese ships brought increasing quantities of pepper, sugar, cinnamon, rice, tea, cotton cloth, and other products to Europe. Payment was made in silver or in European wines and metals. The Portuguese converted many people in India to Christianity.

The great profits made by the Portuguese led the Dutch, the French, and the English to challenge their monopoly. The Portuguese could not stand the strong competition and greater naval and military power of their rivals and were forced gradually to yield their areas of influence in India. They kept Goa, however, until 1961.

BRITISH EXPANSION

The trading posts that ultimately became the centers of power in India and other Asiatic countries were not established by the governments of the European countries. They were the commercial enterprise of private trading companies established by businesses to make money.

Such a company was the British East India Company, which in 1600 was given a monopoly on British trade with India, China, and the East Indies. The company was given power to sign treaties with Indian rulers, to maintain armies to protect growing trade, and to govern by itself.

The company set up a trading post on the southwest coast in 1612. Forts were soon built at Madras, Bombay, and Calcutta. Gradually around each post a town grew up, which attracted more and more Indians who worked as agents or servants of the company.

Clash with the French. A French East India Company, formed in 1664, established a trading post on the southeast coast of India at Pondichéry (pawn-dee-shay-REE). It carried on business with local rulers and employed Indian soldiers. Indians serving in the army of a European country were called **sepoys.**

During the 18th century, Mogul rule weakened. New kingdoms under new rulers fought for power. The British and French, to strengthen their trade position, looked for allies among these warring Indian powers.

France and Britain were at war in Europe, North America (the French and Indian War), and in India. Despite the negotiation of peace in Europe, hostilities persisted in India. The French were finally defeated, and the governor of Pondichéry, Joseph Dupleix (doo-PLEKS), recalled to France.

The person responsible for the ultimate victory of the British in India was Robert Clive. In 1751, when French-supported Indian rulers threatened to defeat the company, Clive took command of a small army of several hundred British soldiers and sepoys and captured the city of Arcot (ahr-KAHT), near Madras. In 1757, he achieved an even more remarkable victory at the battle of Plassey, leading 3,200 British troops to victory over 50,000 French soldiers and their Indian allies. The victory at Plassey made it possible for the East India Company to take control of Bengal, at that time the richest province in India. Clive was appointed governor of Bengal.

In 1760 Clive returned to England. In 1765 he returned to India as governor of Bengal and built up British military and economic power in northern and central India. After returning again to England, Clive was accused in 1773 of having accepted bribes from Indian princes and of amassing a huge personal fortune. He defended his actions and was acquitted. However, the trial left him bitter, his health was shattered, and in 1774 he committed suicide.

The Battle of Plassey in June, 1757, opened the way for British control of India and made Robert Clive, top left, a baron. Clive's British troops, top right, soundly defeated a combined Indian-French force, despite the Indians' use of mobile artillery and elephants, above.

Reasons for British Success in India. The British succeeded in bringing all of India under their direct or indirect control, a feat no other ruler of India had ever accomplished. The British succeeded for the following reasons:

- The collapse of the Mogul empire left India divided and disorganized. Indian rulers fought each other for control of small areas.

- The British used a policy of "divide and conquer." They allied themselves with small states against larger ones. They supported one ruler against another. They played on the weaknesses of local rulers. These tactics allowed them to gradually extend their control.

- British superiority in military and naval power enabled them to defeat larger armies than their own. They trained and equipped sepoys with modern weapons.

- A series of able administrators and governors introduced reforms and improved local government services.

Later Governors-General. During his term as governor of Bengal (1772–1785) and then as the first governor-general of India, Warren Hastings reformed the government of his territory. He laid the foundations for the **Indian Civil Service**, the organization of nonmilitary employees of the East India Company. He organized a system of law courts open to all the subjects in the company's territories. He abolished internal **tariffs**, or taxes on imports and exports, so that goods could pass freely throughout the area.

The company was faced with problems from three neighboring states: Mysore (meye-SOHR), Hyderabad, and the Maratha Confederacy, all surrounding the southeastern possessions of the company. Hastings supported first one, then another of the opponents so that, although outnumbered, the British lost no territory. Three years after his return to England, Hastings, like Clive, was charged with corruption in his Indian activities. He, too, was found not guilty after a long, bitter trial, but it cost him his fortune and his health.

It had long been the practice for company officials to engage in businesses of their own on the side. Their salaries were low, the riches of India were vast, and the opportunities for enriching themselves were indeed great. All this ended with the governorship of Lord Cornwallis (1786–1793), better remembered by Americans as the British general who was defeated at Yorktown in the American Revolution. He reformed the Indian Civil Service, prohibited the employees from engaging in trade for their own benefit, and raised salaries to make employment more attractive. As part of his reform program, Cornwallis denied to Indians the higher posts of government, in the belief that they were responsible for much of the corruption in the company's affairs.

His successor, Lord Wellesley (1798–1805), defeated the Nizam (ruler) of Hyderabad and the Sultan of Mysore, allies of the French. He annexed the territories of several lesser rulers who were too weak to resist him. On others he forced alliances that left them dependent on British support. By the time he had left his position, the East India Company was no longer just a trading company. It had become the strongest power in India.

The extension of company rule into central India was continued by Lord Hastings, governor-general from 1813 to 1823. The western part of Nepal in the north was annexed. His successor, Lord Amherst (1823–1828), annexed Assam in the northeast and conducted a successful war against the king of Burma.

Lord Bentinck introduced some significant Western ideas during his term as governor-general (1828–1835). English was made the official language for all Indian matters. He abolished the practice of *suttee*, according to which some Hindu widows threw themselves onto the funeral pyres of their dead husbands and thus joined them in death. He stamped out the murderous fanatics called *thugs*, a word that has come into the English language. The practice of female infanticide (the killing of girl babies) was stopped.

Under Lord Dalhousie (dal-HOO-zih) from 1848 to 1856, the process of British conquest was completed. The Punjab and Burma were annexed, as were the great state of Oudh and a number of small Maratha states whose rulers died without heirs.

During Lord Dalhousie's term of office, a postal service and telegraph system were set up. Roads and railroads were constructed on a national scale. Canals for irrigation, particularly the Ganges Canal, provided a steady supply of water for farming purposes. By a law of 1854, a Department of Public Instruction was established in every province to promote elementary education in the native language and higher education in English. Girls as well as boys were to receive this education. Vocational, medical, and engineering schools were improved, and private ownership of land was introduced.

Gradual Expansion of Parliamentary Control. The East India Company's power and wealth led to demands that the British

Parliament take over the company's possessions in India. In 1773, Parliament for the first time asserted the right to regulate the company by appointing its own governor-general. In 1784, a new Regulating Act created a Board of Control under Parliamentary supervision, with authority to recall a governor-general and to supervise all the acts that "relate to the civil or military government, or the revenues of the British territorial possessions in the East Indies."

In 1813, Parliament ended the company's monopoly on Indian trade. In 1833, it deprived the company of trading rights in India but kept it as the British government's agent as ruler of India. In 1853, Parliament ended the company's power to appoint whoever it liked to the civil service, requiring instead that entry to the service be based on competitive examinations.

THE GREAT UPRISING OF 1857

A year after Lord Dalhousie had returned to England, the discontent of Indian troops came to violence. In May 1857, what the British call the "Sepoy Mutiny" or the "Great Indian Mutiny" took place. Some Indians call it the "First War of Indian Independence."

The revolt began in the army post at Meerut (MAY-ruht), some 30 miles (48 km) from Delhi. There the company's sepoys killed every European man, woman, and child on whom they could lay their hands. News of this quickly spread, and the sepoys at the army posts in Kanpur and Lucknow also mutinied.

The immediate cause of the revolt was the issuing of new cartridges that had been greased with animal fat. The soldier had to bite off the end of the cartridge and pour the powder into the barrel of his gun. Since to Hindus the cow was sacred, touching cartridges greased with beef fat was a sacrilege. Among Islamic soldiers, it was rumored that the cartridges were greased with pork, which to them was forbidden.

Another cause of resentment was the requirement that soldiers serve outside India, even though travel across ocean waters was regarded as wrong by upper-caste Hindus. The new railroad and telegraph construction was disturbing also, and there were rumors of enforced conversion to Christianity. Underlying all other causes was the growing fear that the British were destroying traditional Indian culture.

The revolt received support from many discontented elements in northern India—dispossessed princes, their unemployed former soldiers, and many others who were worried over the introduction of foreign

Indian cavalry, left, attack British infantry at Kanpur during the Great Uprising of 1857.

ideas and the outlawing of old Indian customs. Yet the uprising did not spread throughout India. South India did not join it, and even in the north many remained on the British side. These included the Sikhs, who resented their treatment by the Muslims of India more than they did their treatment by the British.

The mutiny was defeated only after a year of hard fighting and only with the help of British troops from abroad. The British suppression of the revolt was as cruel and as violent as had been its beginnings. The entire population of Delhi, for example, was driven from the city, and thousands were killed, many without any kind of trial.

THE BRITISH RAJ

When the revolt had finally been put down, the British government decided to take over the company's empire. In 1858, Parliament passed "An Act for the Better Government of India," which transferred the entire administration of the company to the British government. This British Government of India came to be known as the *Raj* (RAHJ), a term derived from the Hindi word for *kingdom*.

The Government of India.   India under the Raj was divided into two unequal parts: British India and Native India. British India, under control of Parliament, consisted of about three-fifths of the subcontinent, including the most heavily populated and productive areas. Native India consisted of about one-third of the land and about one-fourth of the population in 562 princely states. These were scattered over the subcontinent, and ranged in size from Hyderabad, as large as France, to tiny states of a few hundred acres. Some states were ruled by Hindu rulers called *maharajahs*, others by Islamic rulers called *nawabs* or *nizams*.

The princes' powers were regulated by treaties with either the East India Company or the British government. Some were allowed to control their own courts, schools, and even soldiers. However, the British government was in charge of their foreign affairs and their relations

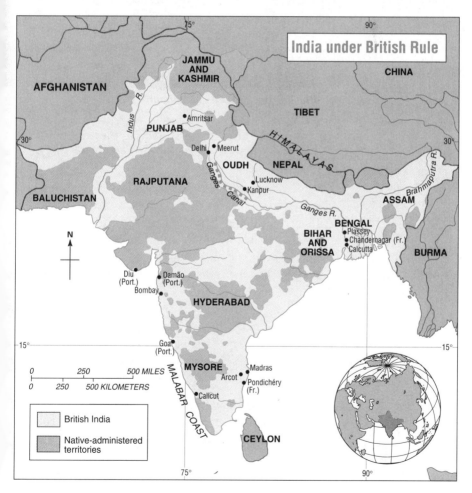

A statue of Britain's Queen Victoria in front of a public building in Calcutta stands as a reminder of the years that India was part of the British Empire.

with one another. It even had the right to supervise their internal affairs. Each Indian ruler was advised by a British official called a *resident*, who was appointed by the viceroy.

In 1876, by an act of Parliament, Queen Victoria was made Empress of India and ruler over the Indian princes' states as well as British India. At the head of the government was the viceroy, appointed by the British government and responsible to the Secretary of State for India, and to Parliament. He governed with the help of appointed officials, mostly British. The chief posts in the Indian government were filled by men hand-picked from the Indian Civil Service, which, despite its name, was made up mainly of British citizens. As late as 1935, only one-third were Indian. The Indians under the Raj had almost no voice in the government of their states or country. Elective positions were few, and no elections were held until the 20th century, when the British began to yield to Indian demands that they control their own destiny.

Benefits of British Rule.   During the many years of British control, significant changes were brought about in Indian life, thought, and work, among them the following:

- India, for the first time in its history, was largely unified. With this Pax Britannica ("British Peace") came a greater degree of peace, law and order, and political unity than the Indian people had known since the time of Asoka, more than 2,000 years before.

- Concrete improvements included the following:

  (a) The best and most extensive railroad system in all of Asia was constructed. Its 4,000 miles of railroad track in 1871 had in creased to 40,000 miles by 1941.

  (b) A national postal and telegraph network had been established.

  (c) A canal system helped irrigate and reclaim millions of acres of land for agriculture.

  (d) Public health measures against cholera, smallpox, and other deadly diseases helped lower the death rate. The population of India increased from 100 million in the 17th century to 300 million at the beginning of the 20th century.

  (e) A famine relief system aided millions of starving people when harvests were poor. It is estimated that 20 million people starved during drought years in the 19th century.

- New schools were started by the British, by princely governments, by missionaries, and by private enterprise. These schools were at all

A siding on a British-built Indian railroad in the 1880s. This scene is in the West Punjab near Lahore, in present-day Pakistan.

levels, including universities. The English language was used in all schools of higher education. Though only a tiny minority of Indians attended these schools, those who did received a good British education. Facility in English became the badge of educated persons. They studied English ideas about democracy and nationalism, and from among them eventually came the leaders of the movement for Indian independence.

- Law and order were established by a competent group of civil servants, who accustomed the people to British processes of government.

- The ideal of equality before the law, regardless of religion, race, or social status, was introduced to India (although ironically the British did not practice it themselves in their dealing with Indians).

- Certain practices were ended, including suttee and female infanticide.

- Textile and jute factories and iron and steel plants were built, marking the beginning of industrialism. Shipping and banking facilities were expanded, as was trade with the rest of the world.

Limitations of British Rule. Many Indians and others believe that India's present poverty is due to the fact that the British drained great wealth from the country and used the Indian economy for the benefit of Britain rather than India.

The concrete improvements noted above, they say, were paid for entirely by the Indian taxpayers. Even the maintenance of the British army in India was paid out of local taxes. (In 1776, British attempts to impose this same policy on the 13 American colonies had been one of the causes of the American Revolution.) Famines were caused by the British diversion of farmlands to the growing of commercial crops for sale outside India.

One of the most serious complaints against the British during their period of control was the almost complete separation of ruler from ruled. Indians were barred from senior positions in the Civil Service. The British treated the Indians as inferiors socially, morally, and culturally. Indians were barred from membership in British clubs. The British attitude toward Indian customs and religions ranged from disapproval to contempt. The British developed a caste system of their own, summarized by signs saying "For Europeans Only" that were posted in public places such as railway carriages, park benches, and restaurants.

CASE STUDY:

Officers in the Indian Army

Relations between the British and the Indians often were difficult. Misunderstandings were common. Changes did occur, however, and some of them were for the better. One area of change was the Indian army.

> The "Indianization" of the Indian Civil Service and the Indian Army had been put . . . [into effect] immediately after the end of the Great War [World War I], but in the Indian Army it was not sincerely applied. To avoid having British officers serving under Indians, special segregated units were set up. In Claude Auchinleck's opinion this had "a very bad effect on Indian feelings. The Indian officers themselves realized that they were being put into units which might be reckoned as inferior to the British officers' units. The only result was that these Indian regiments became objects of contempt."
>
> The establishment of an Indian "Sandhurst" [military academy, like West Point in the United States] did much to improve matters. "I regard my time at the Indian Military Academy as a watershed," states Reginald Savory, one of its first instructors, "not only in my military career but in my political thinking. For the first time I met young, middle-class Indians on level terms and I found all these young men fascinating. They were very outspoken, highly intelligent, and one of the first remarks I had levelled at me was this, 'You British officers of the Indian Army don't know India. All you know are your servants and your sepoys.'"

Charles Allen, editor. *Plain Tales from the Raj: Images of British India in the Twentieth Century.* New York: St. Martin's Press, 1975.

1. What kind of segregation was there in the Indian army?

2. What were the effects of this segregation?

3. How did the establishment of a military academy lead to improved British-Indian understanding?

The small home industries of spinning and weaving cotton cloth, which had been an important way of earning a living for many Indians, were ruined by the competition of British machine-made textiles. British industry was protected against the manufactured imports of India, but no tariff was placed on British goods coming into India until 1921. This policy, by making British manufactured goods cheaper than Indian handmade ones, put millions of artisans in the cities and towns out of work, driving them back to the villages and into poverty.

The landholding and tax-collecting systems helped make the Indian peasants poor. The British introduced the system of paying taxes in cash instead of in a percentage of the crop raised. When the harvest was bad, the peasant, unable to pay in cash, was faced with the prospect of losing his land. This forced him to borrow the money to pay his taxes, putting a burden on him that often remained for the rest of his life. In the northern part of India, tax collectors called *zamindars* (zuh-meen-DAHRZ) became landlords at the expense of the peasants in their districts. The tax collectors grew rich while the peasants became either sharecroppers on land that was formerly theirs, or unemployed. Some farmers had to take jobs building canals, collecting firewood, or working on the land of the rich farmers as part-time workers. This system increased the poverty of the Indian people.

Summary. It is not easy to assess the good and the bad results of British rule in India. There were many positive achievements, as we have seen. But there were also effects from which the Indian people have not yet recovered. Underlying everything was the basic fact that foreigners ruled India instead of Indians themselves.

However, journalists, teachers, and lawyers had been trained in British universities. The movement for Indian independence would probably have unfolded differently without the free press and the training in law that the British allowed in India. Indians also were trained for government in the civil service, though their positions were on the lower levels. A group of well-trained officials was ready to carry on government when the day of freedom came, and meanwhile the ideas of nationalism and democracy united Indians against British imperialism.

REVIEWING THE CHAPTER

I. **Building Your Vocabulary**

In your notebook, write the correct term that matches the definition.

viceroy	resident	sepoy
zamindar	raj	Pax Britannica

1. British official who advised a local Indian ruler

2. Indian serving in the British army

3. the British government in India

4. a tax collector who became a landlord

5. the highest British official in India

II. **Understanding the Facts**

In your notebook, write the numbers from 1 to 5. Write the letter of the correct answer to each question next to its number.

1. Who made the first permanent European settlement in India?
   a. the French   b. the British   c. the Portuguese

2. Where was the chief Portuguese trading port in India located?
   a. Calcutta   b. Pondichéry   c. Goa

3. Which of the following was one of the first British trading ports in India?
   a. Pondichéry   b. Calcutta   c. Surat

4. What term was used for Indian soldiers?
   a. sepoys   b. nizams   c. nawabs

5. How much of India did British India occupy during the period of Parliamentary control?
   a. the greater part of the country
   b. a small part of the country
   c. only the least important parts of the country

III. Thinking It Through

In your notebook, write the numbers from 1 to 5. Write the letter of the correct conclusion to each sentence next to its number.

1. The European nation that maintained a monopoly on trade with India in the 16th century was:
   a. France.   b. Britain.
   c. Portugal.   d. the Netherlands.

2. The trading posts of the British East India Company most close-ly resembled:
   a. small encampments on a harbor, with several houses, offices, and warehouses.
   b. armed towns populated by many sepoys and Indian employ-ees of the British.
   c. certain streets in Indian harbor towns known to be the "British" location.
   d. large palaces guarded by troops loyal to the local Indian ruler.

3. The revolt of the sepoys in 1857 was sparked by:
   a. new cartridges that had been greased with animal fat.
   b. the creation of canals along the Ganges River.
   c. the use of the English language for all Indian matters by the British East India Company.
   d. British refusal to promote sepoys.

4. The Indian Civil Service during British control:
   a. accepted Indians and Britons in all positions.
   b. excluded Indians from high positions.
   c. favored Muslims over Hindus for high positions.
   d. favored Hindus over Muslims for high positions.

5. As a result of British occupation, the Indian home textile indus-try:
   a. prospered as a result of new equipment and the opening of new European markets.
   b. collapsed because Indians could choose more profitable occu-pations.
   c. was protected under British law from competition.
   d. collapsed under the competition of British machine-made tex-tiles and the British-imposed tariffs on Indian imports.

DEVELOPING CRITICAL THINKING SKILLS

1. How might the history of the British in India have been different if the Mogul Empire had been at its height in 1760?

2. Explain how a relatively small British force, far from home, was able to take over all of India.

3. Describe three major ways in which British rule over India was beneficial to Indians and three major ways in which it was harmful. Overall, do you think that British rule did more harm to India or more good? Explain your answer.

4. How might schools established and maintained in India by the British contribute to the growth of an Indian independence movement?

INTERPRETING A GRAPH

Study the graph below and answer the following questions. Write the answers in your notebook.

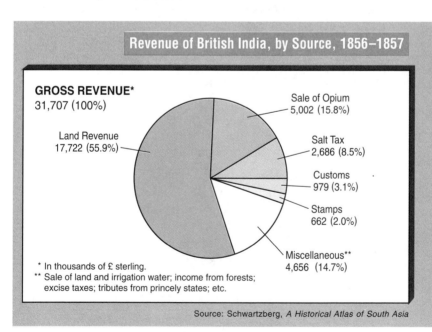

Revenue of British India, by Source, 1856–1857

GROSS REVENUE*
31,707 (100%)

Land Revenue
17,722 (55.9%)

Sale of Opium
5,002 (15.8%)

Salt Tax
2,686 (8.5%)

Customs
979 (3.1%)

Stamps
662 (2.0%)

Miscellaneous**
4,656 (14.7%)

* In thousands of £ sterling.
** Sale of land and irrigation water; income from forests; excise taxes; tributes from princely states; etc.

Source: Schwartzberg, *A Historical Atlas of South Asia*

89

1. Write one sentence explaining what the graph illustrates.
2. How much total revenue did the British obtain from India in 1856–1857?
3. From what source did the British obtain most of their revenue?
4. What major event in the history of India occurred in 1857?

INTERPRETING A CARTOON

Study the cartoon on the facing page and answer the following questions. Write the answers in your notebook.

1. The woman in the cartoon is Queen Victoria of Great Britain. The peddler is British Prime Minister Disraeli, who encouraged Victoria to accept the title "Empress of India." Disraeli is portrayed as the evil uncle in the story *Aladdin and His Wonderful Lamp*. Why did Aladdin's uncle wish to exchange "new lamps for old"? (Review the story if necessary.) What is the cartoonist's opinion of Disraeli's new crown?

2. Study the drawing of Queen Victoria. Write a statement about the cartoonist's opinion of Victoria.

ENRICHMENT AND EXPLORATION

1. Draw two cartoons illustrating the great wealth brought to Great Britain by British rule in India. Draw one cartoon from the British point of view. Show the Indian point of view in your second cartoon.

2. Read one of the short stories that the English writer Rudyard Kipling wrote about India, such as "Wee Willie Winkie." What does Kipling's writing reveal about the attitude of the British towards India and the Indians? Write a short report about the attitudes and behavior of the British in India as portrayed by Kipling, giving examples from the story. Give examples also of how Kipling portrays Indians.

3. Prepare a chart showing the changes and reforms introduced by Hastings, Cornwallis, Bentinck, and Dalhousie. Use the headings *Name of Leader*, *Dates of Office*, and *Changes and Reform*.

"NEW CROWNS FOR OLD"

INDIA AND THE WORLD
1885–Today

1885	Indian National Congress is organized.
1906	All-India Muslim League is founded.
1909	Morley–Minto reforms
1914–1918	*World War I*
1919	Amritsar Massacre
1921	Mohandas Gandhi's first campaign of civil disobedience
1930	Mohandas Gandhi's Salt March
1935	Government of India Act
1939–1945	*World War II*
1947	Mountbatten becomes viceroy. India partitioned into India and Pakistan. Independence of both countries, August 15 Conflict over Kashmir begins.
1947–1964	Nehru serves as prime minister.
1948	Mohandas Gandhi assassinated. India invades and takes over Hyderabad.
1949	Cease-fire in Kashmir
1949	*People's Republic of China is proclaimed.*
1964–1966	Lal Bahadur Shastri is prime minister.
1965–1966	War between India and Pakistan over Kashmir
1966–1967	Indira Gandhi is prime minister.
1975	Indira Gandhi declares state of emergency.
1977–1980	Morarji Desai is prime minister.
1980	Indira Gandhi returns as prime minister.
1984	Indira Gandhi is assassinated.
1984–1989	Rajiv Gandhi succeeds his mother as prime minister.
1991	Rajiv Gandhi is assassinated.
	Soviet Union collapses.

5 Independence For India

The British created a united India, an India in which one language, English, was spoken by all its educated people. They built a railroad system that crisscrossed the country and helped bring people together. They established a single law and a single government. The schools taught Western ideas of democracy, unification, and independence through courses in history and literature. All of these developments contributed to growing nationalist feelings in India.

THE GROWTH OF NATIONALISM

An interest in and a love of their own country gradually awakened among Indians. They began to think of themselves as being Indians, and became proud of their heritage, whether they were Hindu or Muslim, Brahman or outcaste, rich or poor. This feeling of unity was strengthened by growing resentment of the British, which provided a common bond among all groups.

Formation of the Congress Party. Under the leadership of a retired Englishman, Allan O. Hume, a group of Indians organized the Indian National Congress in 1885. The organization is also referred to as the "Congress Party," or simply "the Congress." Its first meeting was attended by 70 people, most of them from the professional and intellectual class. Sympathetic Britons lent their support. Three of them were elected to the presidency of the party in the early years of its history.

The Congress met every year in a different city. Before 1900 it grew slowly. Thereafter, its membership began to increase more rapidly. It was controlled by moderates whose chief demands were for greater Indian participation in the government, the holding of civil service examinations in India as well as in London, wider employment of Indians in the public services, and an increased educational program.

The leader of the moderates was Gopal K. Gokhale (GOH-kah-lawn). As president of the Congress in 1905, he favored a slow, peaceful path to freedom and supported a program of social welfare.

Not all Indian leaders were so moderate in their demands. Bal G. Tilak, a religious leader from the Western Ghats, preached noncoopera-tion with the British and advocated terrorism and violence. He spent a number of years in jail for the murder of British officials.

Muslims as well as Hindus were members of the Congress Party during those early years and combined their efforts to secure more free-dom for the Indians. However, in 1906, the All India Muslim League was created because Muslims feared the domination of the Hindu majority. The Aga Khan, hereditary ruler of the Muslims and well known in Europe, was influential in its formation. Sometimes the two organizations supported each other, but more often each tried to pre-vent the other from becoming too strong in areas where religious feel-ings were high.

First British Government Reforms (1909). A series of events in the early years of the 20th century created much unrest in India. Epidemics of bubonic plague and influenza and droughts killed millions of people. Lord Curzon, the viceroy, increased government control over Indian universities to raise academic standards. This led to protests from disap-pointed students. In 1905 he partitioned the large province of Bengal to improve the efficiency of local administration. The eastern section, many of whose people were Muslims, was joined to the province of Assam. Many Hindus objected to this move, and revolts broke out in which some British officials were killed.

The British Parliament decided to take action. In 1909 it adopted the Morley–Minto Reforms. These provided for an increase in the elect-ed membership of the imperial legislative council. They also permitted separate representation for Muslims, thus foreshadowing the later democratic development along religious lines with Hindus and Muslims voting for candidates of their own faith in proportion to their popula-tion.

Weaknesses of Indian Nationalism. The Indian independence move-ment before World War I was weak, not because of its moderate demands, but because of (1) conflicts between the Hindu majority and the Islamic minority, and (2) the narrowness of its base. The movement was built essentially on the Western-educated middle class, whose members were more concerned with gaining political rights for themselves than in doing anything about the economic needs of the millions of peasants whose situation was getting worse and worse.

India and the First World War.   Although Britain was fighting Turkey in World War I, and the ruler of Turkey was the nominal head of the Islamic religion, the Indian Muslims did not turn on the British. In fact, all classes and groups in India, with few exceptions, supported the British cause wholeheartedly. The Muslim League and the Indian National Congress voted loyalty. More than one million Indians served in the British army in various parts of the world. Indian princes contributed generous sums of money to the British. From India came increased supplies of wheat and other foodstuffs for the British people.

The Fourteen Points of the U.S. President, Woodrow Wilson, calling for "self-determination for all peoples," fired hopes for independence. The Russian Revolution of 1917, in which the despotic imperial government of the czar was overthrown, deepened the conviction that freedom was possible.

Montagu–Chelmsford Reforms, 1919.   After the end of the war in 1918, unrest increased as Indian leaders made increasingly strong demands for reforms. The British responded by adopting the Montagu–Chelmsford Reforms in 1919. These reforms increased the degree of self-government in the Indian provinces through a dual system known as *dyarchy* (DY-ar-kee). The provincial legislatures, in which Indians were in the majority, were given control of education, agriculture, and public health in their territories. A federal legislative Assembly was elected by a greatly increased electorate (5 million voters qualified). However, the British viceroy retained control over the important areas of finance, taxation, police, foreign trade, and foreign policies.

Political and social unrest continued to flare up in various parts of India as demands for complete independence grew louder. To fight these "fires," the British adopted the Rowlatt laws, giving judges the power to try political cases without juries and giving provincial governments the power to intern suspects without trial. Widespread indignation and protests followed.

One such protest meeting was held at Amritsar (um-RIT-ser) in the Punjab in April 1919. British troops fired without warning on the unarmed Indians. At least 380 Indians were killed and 1,200 were wounded. The massacre shocked many Indians who until then had taken little interest in politics. It brought a new leader into Indian politics, Mohandas K. Gandhi (MOH-han-dahs GAHN-dee).

GANDHI (1869–1948)

His Early Life. Gandhi was born of a Hindu family in the state of Gujarat on the western coast of India. His father and grandfather had been prime ministers in small states in the region, although the family belonged to a Vaisya, or merchant, caste. He learned from his mother to appreciate *ahimsa*, nonviolence to all living things. He was married at 13 to a girl of his own age.

At the age of 18, he was sent to England to continue his studies. Three years later, he graduated with a law degree and returned to India. He left shortly afterward for South Africa, where thousands of Indian immigrants offered possibilities of work for a young lawyer willing to live abroad, and he stayed there until 1915. In South Africa he was successful in furthering the rights of the small Indian minority, which was being discriminated against.

Gandhi's Methods. It was in India that Gandhi put into operation his idea of mass resistance through nonviolence. He called this *satyagraha* (SUHT-yuh-gruh-huh), or "soul force". This force came from Gandhi's belief that it was wrong to injure a living being, that love should be returned for hate, good for evil, unselfishness for selfishness. He believed in conquering by the power of goodness. His idea was that an

Wearing only a simple loin cloth, Mohandas Gandhi explains his principles. Gandhi showed India and the world the power of moral persuasion through nonviolent civil disobedience.

opponent could be won over more surely by love, patience, and sympathy than by force.

He urged a program of noncooperation and civil disobedience. He said: "Don't pay your taxes or send your children to an English-supported school. Send them to a school where they may learn their own native language. Make your own cotton cloth by spinning the thread at home, and don't buy English-made goods. Provide yourselves with homemade salt, and do not buy government-made salt." He argued for a better status for untouchables, renaming them *harijans*, or "children of God." "I do not want a kingdom, salvation, or heaven," he said. "What I want is to remove the troubles of the oppressed and the poor." He favored more freedom for women, a return to the ideals of ancient Hinduism, and the improvement of village economics. He wanted nothing for himself. He dressed in the peasant's homespun loin cloth, or *dhoti* (DOH-tee). He became a strict vegetarian, eating barely enough to keep alive. He fasted for penance and also to secure political concessions from the British government. By his beliefs, his actions, his very life, he was considered a saint by his people. His leadership in their drive toward complete independence increased steadily after 1920.

Gandhi contributed the following to Indian nationalism:

- He introduced the highly successful methods of nonviolent noncooperation and civil disobedience.

- He changed the base of the movement for complete independence from a small Western-educated group into a mass movement supported by millions.

- He brought into the nationalist movement the concepts of social justice and equality.

The Indian people called Gandhi, with great affection, *Mahatma* (ma-HAT-ma), meaning "great soul." Sometimes they added -*ji* to his name to show the respect in which he was held: *Gandhiji*. Sometimes he was referred to as *Bapu*, meaning "father," or *Bapuji*, "honored father."

Beginnings of Noncooperation.   Gandhi at first favored cooperation with the British. But after the Amritsar Massacre in 1919, he turned his back on them and embarked on a countrywide tour calling upon the people to boycott English goods, schools, and courts, and to refuse to pay taxes. Millions of Indians, from peasants to students and Congress leaders, followed his lead. The movement did not succeed. Violence broke out, and Gandhi called off his noncooperation campaign. He was put in jail by the British, the first of several sentences he served.

For the next few years, Gandhi continued his efforts to teach the Indians how to use his methods more effectively. He talked, he fasted, he taught. More and more Indians listened to him. More and more of the British in India and in Britain began to realize that their days of empire in India were drawing to a close.

A sign of this was revealed in the Simon Commission Report in 1929, which recommended increased responsibility for the elected provincial legislatures and eventual dominion status for India. Because there had been no Indians on this commission, the Indian National Congress boycotted its report and issued a declaration of independence setting January 26, 1930, as Independence Day. It was 20 years later to the day that the Constitution of Free India finally came into effect. The date is now celebrated annually as Republic Day, the Indian equivalent of the U.S. Fourth of July.

To dramatize Indian discontent with the Simon Report in a nonviolent way, Gandhi said he would make tax-free salt on the seashore in defiance of the British salt monopoly. He left his *ashram*, or retreat, near Ahmedabad and walked 241 miles in 24 days, with an ever-increasing group of followers. This Salt March, which was reported in the world's newspapers, was followed by wide-scale and effective civil disobedience. In less than a year 60,000 people were put in jail. But the salt tax was not repealed.

Conferences were held in London, which Gandhi was invited to attend. On the promise that political prisoners would be released, Gandhi went to London. When he returned to India to learn that repressive laws were still being enforced, he resumed civil disobedience. Tens of thousands of Indians followed his lead.

This pressure forced Britain to grant further concessions to the Indian nationalists. The Government of India Act of 1935 gave complete autonomy to the provinces and created a federal system by which dominion status was to be achieved later. The franchise was extended to 35 million voters, a large increase over the previous franchise. The central legislature was to consist of representatives from British India and the princely states. It would have wider powers, except that defense and foreign affairs were to be left in the hands of the viceroy. This federal system could not go into effect without the agreement of half the princes. Their agreement was never secured, so the system was never put into operation.

The Indian Congress Party won majorities in the 1937 elections in eight of the 11 provinces of British India. Islamic ministries or coalition governments were formed in the others. This led to bitter feelings between Hindus and Muslims. The Muslim League, under Muhammad Ali Jinnah (1876–1948), a Bombay lawyer and onetime nationalist, split with the Indian National Congress. Jinnah raised the cry, "Islam is in danger!" His demands for an independent Islamic state for the millions of Muslims laid the foundations for what was later to become Pakistan.

India in World War II. World War II, which broke out in 1939, had important effects on India. The country, because of its ties to Britain, found itself at war with Germany and Japan. Indian leaders sympathized with the British cause, but they refused to give official support so long as Britain was unwilling to grant dominion status to India. Many of the Congress leaders went to jail because of their noncooperative attitude. Britain granted them freedom after World War II.

Over 2 million Indian soldiers fought for the British in the war. India raised food and provided war materials for Britain. In 1943, when Britain diverted food from India to soldiers in Burma, the resulting Great Bengali Famine took more than a million lives. At the same time, U.S. air bases, troops, and money appeared in India. The unexpected money from the United States enabled India to wipe out its debt to Britain. In fact, by the time the war was over, Britain owed much money to India.

New industries had been created, and many of the established textile and jute mills and iron-processing factories had been transferred to Indian hands. There were many new opportunities for work in factories and in the army. Farmers had more money because of war purchases for the British and U.S. troops. This economic improvement affected the lives and thoughts of millions of Indians.

THE WINNING OF INDEPENDENCE

World War II ended in 1945. European empires in Africa and Asia were breaking up. The Labor Party won the election of 1945 in Britain. Clement Attlee, the new prime minister, was sympathetic toward the idea of an independent India.

The Partition of India. The British faced a serious problem: should India be united or divided? Muhammad Ali Jinnah, leader of the Muslim

99

In Karachi, Lord Louis Mountbatten, last Viceroy of India, salutes at the ceremony at which Pakistan became an independent nation. Lady Mountbatten stands at the right.

League, favored a separate Islamic state to include those parts of India, such as the Punjab in the northwest and Bengal in the east, where the Muslims were in the majority. However, within these provinces there were large areas with Hindu majorities. What protection would be given to minority groups in provinces that were overwhelmingly Hindu or Muslim?

The British suggested a federation of all Indians, with local self-government in minority areas. This set off violence and bloodshed between the two groups.

In March 1947, the British government sent to India a new viceroy, Lord Louis Mountbatten. Within a few weeks he had agreed to set August 1947 as the date for independence. Since he could not arrange an agreement between the Muslim League and the Indian National Congress, he recommended that India be divided into two countries, Hindu India and Islamic Pakistan.

Jawaharlal Nehru (jah-WAH-hahr-lahl NAY-roo), successor to Gandhi as the Congress leader, reluctantly accepted partition. In place of one India there would be two nations, India and Pakistan. Gandhi refused to attend the Independence Day celebration, which took place on August 15, 1947.

Mass Migrations. Even before the division of India into two separate nations was official, millions of Indians packed up their belongings in oxcarts and began to move. Muslims sought the provinces assigned to Pakistan. Hindus and Sikhs fled from them. Conflicts between these groups were inevitable. It is estimated that more than one-half million people were killed in these journeys, which continued for years after partition.

The migrants became a problem for both nations, since they had to be housed, fed, and employed. They had to adjust to their new surroundings and pick up the threads of their old lives among strange people. The help given to them by the states of India and Pakistan was a severe drain on the resources of both governments.

Death of Gandhi. In an effort to end the Hindu–Muslim rioting and killings, Gandhi began a fast until death. When the many leaders of the various religious groups promised that they would do their best to restore harmony and peace, he ended his fast. But the rioting and killings continued.

Many Hindus were angry at Gandhi's tolerant attitude toward Muslims and his efforts to make peace with them. A member of a militant extremist Hindu organization, N. V. Godse, assassinated Gandhi at a prayer meeting on January 30, 1948. The gentle Indian leader, who had so strongly opposed violence for half a century, died by violence.

His death was mourned by all of India and by the whole world. But it did not end the troubles.

The Princely States and India. Under the British plan for partition, the 562 states that were not under direct British control were to be joined with Hindu India, Islamic Pakistan, or remain independent according to the wishes of the ruling prince. Most of the princes were persuaded to join either India or Pakistan, whichever part was next to their own territory.

CASE STUDY:
The Light Has Gone Out

Five months after India gained its independence from Great Britain, Mohandas K. Gandhi, the saintly leader of India's independence movement, was assassinated by one of his countrymen. Later that day India's prime minister, Jawaharlal Nehru, who had loved Gandhi as a son, spoke to the nation.

Friends and comrades, the light has gone out of our lives and there is darkness everywhere. I do not know what to tell you and how to say it. Our beloved leader, Bapu as we called him, the Father of the Nation, is no more. Perhaps I am wrong to say that. Nevertheless, we will not see him again as we have seen him for these many years. We will not run to him for advice and seek solace from him, and that is a terrible blow, not to me only, but to millions and millions in this country. And it is a little difficult to soften the blow by any advice that I or anyone else can give you.

The light has gone out, I said, and yet I was wrong. For the light that shone in this country for these many many years will illumine this country for many more years, and a thousand years later, that light will still be seen in this country and the world will see it and it will give solace to innumerable hearts. For that light represented something more than the immediate present, it represented the living, the eternal truths, reminding us of the right path, drawing us from error, taking this ancient country to freedom.

Margaret Cormack and Kiki Skagen, editors. *Voices from India*. New York: Praeger Publishers, 1972, pages 116–117.

1. How does Nehru attempt to soften the blow of Gandhi's death for the people of India?
2. What is the "right path" that Nehru refers to?

The two largest states, Hyderabad and Kashmir, had not joined with either of the new countries when Independence Day came. Hyderabad, with an Islamic ruler but a predominantly Hindu population, was completely surrounded by Indian territory. The Indian army invaded it in 1948, and it was forced to join India.

Kashmir, which has boundaries with both India and Pakistan, was a more complex problem. Its ruler was Hindu, its people mostly Muslims. Tribesmen from Pakistan invaded Kashmir in 1947, and India flew in troops to prevent them from taking it over. A cease-fire was arranged by the United Nations in January 1949. About two-thirds of Kashmir remained in Indian hands, the remainder under Pakistani control.

For years the United Nations has tried to hold a plebiscite in Kashmir, but it has not been able to do so because of India's objections. Fighting between the troops of India and Pakistan broke out over Kashmir in 1965. Another cease-fire, brought about by the United Nations, ended the fighting. Kashmir was again the subject of war in 1971, and serious rioting in 1990 resulted in strong police action by the Indian government.

The New States of India.   When the princely states joined India or Pakistan, they surrendered all their ruling powers in return for an annual allowance based on a certain percentage of the revenues of their states.

The boundaries of these 27 states were not drawn in a logical or convenient way. In 1956 state boundaries in India were redrawn, largely on the basis of regional language. The 27 states were reduced to 14. Since that time, 11 additional states have been created, bringing the total to 25. Most of these new states were formed by dividing a former state or by giving statehood to a territory formerly governed directly by the national government. An exception is the formerly independent Himalayan kingdom of Sikkim, which in 1975 voted in favor of merging with India. The people of India supported this proposal, and the Indian Parliament made Sikkim a state of the Union.

THE GOVERNMENT OF INDIA

The Indian government is patterned mainly after that of Great Britain, but it has some resemblances to the U.S. system.

Parliamentary System.   The most important official is the prime minister, who is the leader of the political party or coalition of parties that

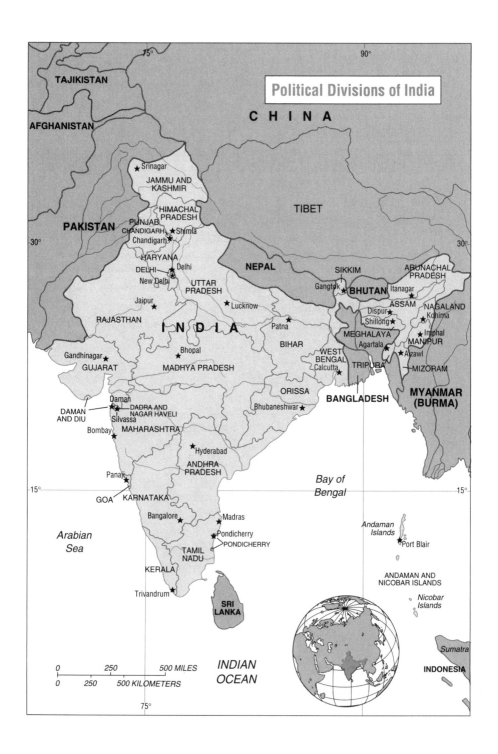

Political Divisions of India

TAJIKISTAN

AFGHANISTAN

C H I N A

Srinagar

JAMMU AND
KASHMIR

HIMACHAL
PRADESH

TIBET

PAKISTAN

PUNJAB
CHANDIGARH ★Shimla
Chandigarh

30°

30°

HARYANA

DELHI   Delhi
New Delhi
UTTAR
PRADESH

NEPAL

SIKKIM

ARUNACHAL
PRADESH

Jaipur   ★Lucknow

Gangtok ★BHUTAN Itanagar

RAJASTHAN

I N D I A

Patna

ASSAM
Dispur★
Shillong★

NAGALAND
★Kohima

Gandhinagar★

Bhopal

BIHAR

MEGHALAYA
Agartala

★Imphal
MANIPUR

GUJARAT

MADHYA PRADESH

WEST
BENGAL
Calcutta

TRIPURA

★Aizawl

MIZORAM

ORISSA

MYANMAR
(BURMA)

Daman

DAMAN
AND DIU

DADRA AND
NAGAR HAVELI
Silvassa

Bhubaneshwar★

BANGLADESH

Bombay★ MAHARASHTRA

★Hyderabad

ANDHRA
PRADESH

Panaji★

Bay of
Bengal

15°

15°

GOA   KARNATAKA

Bangalore★   ★Madras

Andaman
Islands

Arabian
Sea

Pondicherry
PONDICHERRY

TAMIL
NADU

★Port Blair

KERALA

ANDAMAN AND
NICOBAR ISLANDS

Trivandrum★

SRI
LANKA

Nicobar
Islands

Sumatra

0   250   500 MILES

0   250   500 KILOMETERS

INDIAN
OCEAN

INDONESIA

75°

104

controls a majority of the seats in the Lok Sabha (LOHK SAH-bah), the lower house of the Indian Parliament. The prime minister chooses the cabinet, whose members direct the different government departments, such as Foreign Affairs, Education, and Transportation. The cabinet is chosen from the Parliament, and its members remain members of Parliament. If the prime minister should lose the support of the majority in the Lok Sabha, he or she must resign, along with the entire cabinet. If the Lok Sabha cannot then agree on a new prime minister and cabinet, an election must be held to choose new members of the Lok Sabha. In any event, elections must be held at least every five years.

There are a president and a vice president, each of whom is elected for a five-year term by the members of the Indian Parliament and of the state legislatures meeting together. The position of president is largely ceremonial, like that of the British monarch. However, the president does have authority to take over from the prime minister if the prime minister is not able to govern.

The Parliament. The federal legislature consists of two houses. The upper house, Rajya Sabha (RAH-ee-yah SAH-bah), or "Council of States", has 244 members. All but 12 of the members are elected by the state legislatures representing the 25 states. They serve for six years, one third elected every two years (like our Senate). The lower house, Lok Sabha, or "House of the People," has 545 members elected directly for five-year terms by all adults.

On money bills, the Rajya Sabha has only advisory power. On any other bills, if the two houses disagree, a decision is reached by a joint sitting of both houses. This gives greater power to the lower house, which has twice as many members.

As in the U.S. system, there is a Supreme Court that interprets the constitution.

To amend the Indian constitution, two-thirds of the members of each house must be present and vote. A majority of the total membership of each house is needed. Some kinds of amendments must be ratified by the state legislatures. Since 1950, when the constitution came into force, it has been amended 67 times.

The federal government has greater powers than the individual states, which also have parliamentary governments. It can create new states or abolish them, change their boundaries at will, or take over their powers. The federal government controls the major sources of revenue, foreign affairs, defense, interstate commerce, money, highways, and the incorporation of businesses.

105

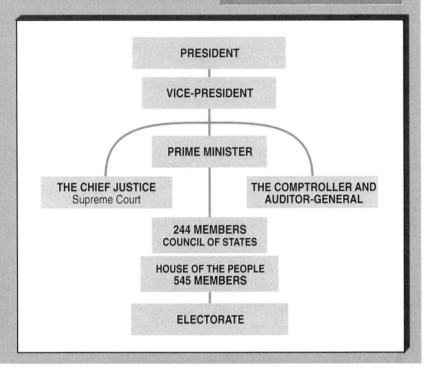

PRESIDENT

VICE-PRESIDENT

PRIME MINISTER

THE CHIEF JUSTICE
Supreme Court

THE COMPTROLLER AND
AUDITOR-GENERAL

244 MEMBERS
COUNCIL OF STATES

HOUSE OF THE PEOPLE
545 MEMBERS

ELECTORATE

The constitution leaves to the states control over police, local government, public health, education, and agriculture. Both state and federal governments have power over prices, treatment of refugees, and the control of professions.

Each state has a governor, appointed by the president of India. The governors have wide powers. They can dismiss the prime minister of their states if they think the public interest demands it. They can dissolve a state legislature before its five-year term is up, order new elections, and veto bills passed by the legislature.

Individual Liberties. The Indian constitution contains an elaborate section on the fundamental rights of all Indians. Freedom of religion is guaranteed, with special protection for religious minorities in cultural and educational matters. Also included among these rights are freedom of speech and association, a guarantee against arbitrary arrest and imprisonment, the outlawing of untouchability, and the forbidding of discrimination of any kind because of race, religion, caste, sex, or place of birth.

Although jury trials are guaranteed for all accused persons, India has a preventive-detention law under which persons who have not yet committed a crime may be put in prison for one they are expected to commit. This law has been applied many times, particularly in 1974–1975, when Prime Minister Indira Gandhi suspended many civil and political rights.

The Indian constitution also contains broad principles of state policy. The slaughter of cattle and the use of intoxicating drinks are prohibited. There are provisions for promoting free and compulsory education for all children under 14, protection of the health and strength of workers, and improvement of the food standards of the people.

Voting in India. There are no educational or literacy requirements for voting in India. All adults are permitted to vote. There are many political parties in India. Since almost half of the voters cannot read or write, how do they know for which party to vote?

Symbols are used to represent the different parties. The Indian National Congress Party is represented by a team of yoked oxen. The Praja Socialist Party's symbol is a thatched hut. Other symbols are a lighted lamp, an elephant, a ladder.

Political Problems. Although there are more than a dozen political parties in India, the Congress Party, the largest before its split, controlled the government until 1977. The elections of February 1967,

Symbols to Represent Different Parties

Political parties are identified for illiterate voters by special symbols.

were, however, disastrous for the party. Although it received more votes than any other party, it won only a narrow majority in the federal legislature. Many voters cast their ballots not so much for an opposition candidate as against the Congress Party candidate. They were protesting food shortages and rising grain prices, riots in many cities, the country's stagnant economy, and the fact that the Congress Party had been so long in office. In 1969 the party suffered more defeats in local elections but retained national office.

In 1975 a court found Indira Gandhi guilty of illegal election practices four years earlier. This setback, combined with an increase in other serious internal opposition, led Gandhi to invoke a state of emergency in June 1975. Free speech was curtailed, and thousands of her political opponents were arrested. These events spurred several opposition parties to merge into the Janata Party which, in the 1977 elections, handed the Congress Party its first-ever election defeat. Morarji Desai, leader of this new group, became Prime Minister.

Disagreements soon developed within the Janata Party. In July 1979, following the resignation from the party of 18 members of Parliament, Desai resigned rather than face a vote of no confidence. Twelve days later, Charan Singh was sworn in as prime minister. However, when Singh failed to gain the support of Indira Gandhi and the opposition political parties, he too was forced to resign. India found itself in political turmoil.

In the 1980 elections, Indira Gandhi returned to power at the head of the reorganized Congress (I) Party—the "I" standing for "Indira"—with an overwhelming majority in both houses of Parliament. A major problem in her second term was increased demands for self-rule by leaders of the Sikhs in the Punjab. At one point she sent troops into the holiest of Sikh temples, an action that resulted in a number of deaths. Two years later, in 1984, Gandhi herself fell victim to Sikh discontent when she was assassinated by two Sikh members of her own bodyguard.

Indira Gandhi was succeeded as prime minister by her son Rajiv. Rajiv Gandhi had entered politics only a few years before, following the death of his brother Sanjay. Rajiv Gandhi remained in power until 1989. In 1991, while campaigning to return as prime minister, he was assassinated. Congress Party leaders tried to convince his Italian-born widow to take Rajiv's place in the party, but she declined to do so. Thus the dynasty that began with Rajiv Gandhi's grandfather, Jawaharlal Nehru, seemed to have come to an end.

After 1989 V.P. Singh and Chandra Sekar served brief terms as prime minister. In 1991 P.V. Narasimha Rao took over the office.

INDIA'S PRIME MINISTERS

Jawaharlal Nehru (1892–1964). In almost every way, Nehru was the opposite of Gandhi. An aristocrat by birth, a member of a wealthy Brahman family, Jawaharlal Nehru was raised in the lap of luxury. At 15 he was sent to England for the best English education, specializing at Cambridge in chemistry, geology, and botany. Then he studied law, was admitted to the bar, and returned to India at the age of 22. His father, Motilal Nehru, a prosperous lawyer, was one of the leaders in the Congress Party, but the son remained aloof from the independence movement until the early 1920s.

The Amritsar Massacre of 1919 (see page 95), followed by Gandhi's first campaign of nonviolent civil disobedience in 1921, made Nehru into an ardent nationalist. He gave up his law practice and devoted all his energies and abilities to the nationalist movement. Like others, he was jailed often for his participation in the civil disobedience campaigns.

He wrote three books while in jail, the quality of which showed him to possess unusual writing talent. One of them, *Glimpses of World History*, written in the form of letters to his daughter Indira, is a study of world history as seen through Asian eyes. An autobiography, *Towards Freedom*, publicized the Indian side of the nationalist struggle and was widely read in many countries. His history of India, *The Discovery of India*, written from a non-British point of view, is considered to be his best book. Nehru came to be referred to as Pandit Nehru, *pandit* meaning "scholar."

Nehru traveled in Europe and Asia when he was not in jail. He visited Russia, Spain, Czechoslovakia, and Italy, observing the operations of both communist and fascist political and economic systems. While he considered fascism the more dangerous evil, his sympathy for communism ended with Russia's treaty with Germany in 1939.

Pandit Nehru became president of the Congress Party in 1929 and was reelected several times. When independence came to India, he was the logical choice to head the new country as its first prime minister. He held the position until his death in January 1964.

During this long period, Nehru successfully led his country through the trials and tribulations of a newborn country. He guided its economy through a series of Five Year Plans intended to improve the people's standards of living, played a leading role in the councils of the United Nations, and raised India's stature among the world's nations. We shall examine some of his work in detail in the next two chapters.

Jawaharlal Nehru, left, India's first prime minister, earned world stature as a leader in the movement for Asian independence. His daughter, Indira Gandhi, below, was India's third prime minister.

Lal Bahadur Shastri (1905–66). After Nehru's death, the Congress Party selected Shastri as its new prime minister. Shastri had been educated in India, not in England, as Gandhi and Nehru had been. He had done no traveling outside of Asia until he took over his new position. However, he had been active in Congress Party politics for many years and had been a member of some of Nehru's cabinets. Because he believed in a "middle of the road" policy, he was chosen as a compromise choice.

The outbreak of war between Pakistan and India in 1965 over Kashmir was an important test of Shastri's government. The cease-fire

Lal Bahadur Shastri, left, served two years as prime minister until his death in 1966. Morarji Desai, right, also served two years, from 1977 to 1979.

that halted the war in a few weeks was followed by a treaty in 1966 between the two countries in which the Soviet Union played a significant role in bringing the leaders of the two countries together at Tashkent, Uzbekistan, in the Soviet Union. Shastri died suddenly a few hours after he had signed the treaty.

Indira Gandhi (1918–1984). The Congress Party chose Nehru's daughter, Indira Gandhi (no relation to the Mahatma), as its new leader. The choice of a woman as the head of the world's largest democratic state suggested the changes and the progress India had made since independence.

In her early years as prime minister, Gandhi survived weakened party influence and disastrous economic conditions. By 1969, however, the Congress Party was in firmer control because of increased food production and a lowered birth rate.

In June 1975, threatened with adverse court rulings in a voting law case, an opposition protest campaign, and strikes, Gandhi invoked emergency provisions of the constitution. Thousands of opponents were arrested, and press censorship was imposed. After resigning from office amid charges of political corruption in 1977, Mrs. Gandhi returned to power in 1980 and continued until her assassination in 1984.

Morarji Desai (1896—). While imprisoned during the national emergency in 1975, Morarji Desai formed the coalition Janata Party to challenge Indira Gandhi. The Janata Party defeated the Congress Party in the 1977 elections and Desai was named Prime Minister. His brief term of office ended with his resignation in 1979, when the Janata Party lost the confidence and support of the people.

111

Rajiv Gandhi speaks to a crowd in southern India shortly after becoming prime minister in 1984.

Rajiv Gandhi (1944–1991).   Rajiv Gandhi was born in Bombay and educated in England. Originally uninterested in a political career, he worked as an airline pilot for nine years after his return to India. Rajiv Gandhi entered Parliament in 1981, the year after the death in a plane crash of his brother Sanjay. In 1983 he was appointed to a high post in the Congress (I) Party and became the party's head after his mother's death the following year.

In 1984 he led Congress (I) to an election victory and served five years as prime minister. During his years in office, his popularity suffered a considerable decline. In 1987 he sent Indian troops to Sri Lanka to help preserve the peace in a civil conflict in that country. He left office in 1989, but decided to attempt a return in 1991. It was while campaigning for that election that he was assassinated by a member of a radical Sri Lankan organization.

P. V. Narasimha Rao (1922–).   Rao took office in 1991, after the brief and troubled periods in office of V. P. Singh and Chandra Shekar. Unrest had increased in Kashmir and the Punjab and had arisen in other parts of India. The economy was in decline. The Soviet Union, India's closest ally, was collapsing. Rajiv Gandhi, who had been expected to return to office, had just been assassinated.

Rao, a former foreign minster, was 69 years old and in poor health. He was a compromise candidate, one who was thought to be not personally ambitious. Yet he surprised observers with the firmness with which he addressed India's problems. The most striking changes were in economic and foreign policy, where he boldly abandoned policies that had been in place for more than 40 years. Before his first year in office had ended, Rao succeeded in bringing India a new hope for the future.

REVIEWING THE CHAPTER

I. **Building Your Vocabulary**

In your notebook, write the correct term that matches the definition.

nonviolence	civil disobedience	Salt March
Muslim League	Amritsar Massacre	*satyagraha*

1. Mohandas Gandhi's dramatic walk to the sea in protest of a British tax

2. political party founded in 1906 to compete with the Hindu-dominated Congress Party

3. Mohandas Gandhi's concept of "soul force," the power of goodness

4. refusal to obey unjust laws as a method of bring reform

5. violent attack by British troops on a protest meeting in the Punjab in 1919

II. **Understanding the Facts**

In your notebook, write the numbers from 1 to 6. Write the letter of the correct answer to each question next to its number.

1. Why did the British jail many Congress leaders during World War II?
   a. They refused official support to the British cause.
   b. They helped Britain's enemies.
   c. They accepted money from Germany.

2. What was the major factor that determined the division of the Indian subcontinent into the nations of India and Pakistan?
   a. language   b. religion
   c. natural barriers, especially mountains

3. What happened to India's princely states upon division?
   a. They were forced to join Pakistan.
   b. They chose to join either Pakistan or India or to remain independent.
   c. They were forced to join India.

4. What is the most powerful office in India today?
   a. viceroy   b. president   c. prime minister

5. How did Prime Minister Indira Gandhi respond to adverse court rulings and public unrest?
   a. She declared a state of emergency and suspended civil rights.
   b. She jailed all the judges involved.
   c. She resigned in favor of her son Rajiv.

6. Which minority group in India has made demands for self-rule?
   a. Christians   b. Buddhists   c. Sikhs

III. Thinking It Through

In your notebook, write the numbers from 1 to 5. Write the letter of the correct conclusion to each sentence next to its number.

1. The first demands of the Congress Party included each of the following items *except*:
   a. greater Indian participation in the government.
   b. full dominion status in the British Commonwealth.
   c. the holding of civil service examinations in India as well as in London.
   d. an increased education program.

2. Before World War I, the Indian independence movement gained most of its support from:
   a. the Western-educated middle class.
   b. the urban poor, including the scheduled classes.
   c. Muslims of eastern Bengal.
   d. Indian princes.

3. Mohandas Gandhi's methods of forcing the British to give India its independence included each of the following *except*:
   a. mass nonviolent resistance.
   b. civil disobedience.
   c. fasting.
   d. full cooperation with British programs.

4. Each of the following was a result of the conflict between Hindus and Muslims in India *except*:
   a. division of India into two nations, India and Pakistan.
   b. annexation of several princely states by neighboring nations.
   c. mass migrations of Hindus and Muslims.
   d. conflict between India and Pakistan over Kashmir.

5. The most powerful part of the government of India is the:
   a. federal government.   b. state governments.
   c. Supreme Court.   d. the *Rajya Sabha*.

DEVELOPING CRITICAL THINKING SKILLS

1. Identify the causes of the growth of Indian nationalism.

2. What effect did the conflict between Hindus and Muslims have on the independence movement?

3. Assess Mohandas Gandhi's contribution to Indian nationalism.

4. Discuss the following statement: "[Indira Gandhi's] place in history remains a matter of controversy. She is blamed for weakening her party, for suspending democracy for nearly two years, for allowing corruption to thrive, for slow economic progress. Yet. . . . She had a remarkable relationship with the people, and this was the bedrock of her considerable popularity and long reign. . . . She embodied the idea of an India united and was a strong-willed figure on the world stage." (Editors of Time-Life Books. *India*. New York: Time-Life Books, 1987, page 101.)

INTERPRETING POLITICAL CARTOONS

Study the cartoons on page 117 and answer the questions that follow. Write the answers in your notebook.

1. Who is the subject of cartoon A?

2. In what two ways might you consider this person a great shadow on the land?

3. Who is the main subject of cartoon B? Why is the subject not shown? What does the whistle symbolize? (The Congress Party's latest symbol is a hand.)

4. What would the artist of cartoon B predict for the future of Indian politics in the mid-1990s?

1. Prepare a short report on the influence of Mohandas Gandhi on Martin Luther King, Jr., the U.S. civil rights leader. Compare the Salt March to the March on Washington held in 1963.

2. Compare the growth of nationalism and the independence movement in India with that of another former colony in Southeast Asia, such as Indonesia or Sri Lanka. Include information about the colonizing nations, the leaders of the independence movements, and the important dates in the independence movement. You may wish to prepare a chart illustrating your findings.

3. Draw a political cartoon about one of the following Indian leaders: Mohandas Gandhi, Muhammad Ali Jinnah, Jawaharlal Nehru, Indira Gandhi. Be prepared to answer questions about your drawing.

4. Write a newspaper article describing (a) Gandhi's Salt March, (b) the assassination of Mohandas Gandhi, (c) the departure of the British from India, or (d) the assassination of Indira Gandhi.

CARTOON A:

CARTOON B:

117

6 India's Economic and Social Challenges

India has a high potential for industrial and electric power development. There are large deposits of high-grade iron ore and coal, important reserves of bauxite (the ore from which aluminum is made), atomic materials like thorium, and large deposits of manganese and mica. The great rivers offer the possibilities of enormous hydroelectric power. India's railroad system is the largest in Asia. India has more irrigated land than any other country in the world. Its population of 844 million people is the second largest in the world.

Yet India remains one of the poorest countries in the world. The average annual income, about $306 in U.S. money, is lower than most countries'. Nearly two-thirds of the Indian people cannot read or write. The great majority of the people lack proper housing, medical care, and education.

Do these paragraphs seem to contradict each other? Let us examine some of the serious challenges that India faces today.

AGRICULTURE

Farming is the most important single occupation of the Indian people. About 70 percent of the Indians are farmers who till their small plots of land in the same way their ancestors before them did. In spite of difficulties, however, they are able to raise enough food for the ever-increasing population.

Problems in Agriculture. Indian agriculture has had to overcome many difficulties:

Many Indian farmers still use the centuries-old method of letting the wind separate chaff from grain.

- **Small Farms.** India's millions of farms are small. Many are no more than two or three acres in size, the average being about 7.5 acres. Much of the food the small farms produce—milk, grain, vegetables, and fruit—is eaten by the farmers and their families, leaving little as a surplus for the city inhabitants.

- **Primitive Tools.** Most farmers use a short-handled hoe and a wooden stick (sometimes with an iron tip) to break the ground for seeding. The steel plow is used on few farms. Although more and more farmers have tractors and rotor tillers, the small size of many farms makes it impractical to use tractors, harvesters, and other large and expensive machines.

- **Low Productivity Per Acre.** Indian farmers are faced with plant diseases and animal pests (rats) that destroy part of their crop every year. Farmers may not have enough storage room to keep their grain safely. Although the supply of fertilizer has improved, in some places it is still inadequate. Many farmers do not have enough water to irrigate the land. As a result, most Indian farmers raise less per acre than in such countries as the United States or Japan.

- **Heavy Debts of the Farmers.** Many farmers are in debt to moneylenders or rich farmers in the neighborhood. Previous crop failures forced them to borrow money to buy seed, food, and clothing. The high interest rates charged by the village moneylenders are a great burden to the poor farmers.

Economic Planning. Shortly after India won its freedom, the government decided to increase food production, develop industries, and raise the standard of living of the people through programs of economic planning—a series of Five Year Plans.

Although India borrowed this idea of economic planning from the Soviet Union, it was carried out by democratic, not dictatorial, means. The programs, covering agriculture, industry, education, irrigation, housing, and public health, were drawn up by groups of experts from the central government, from the state governments, and from private groups. They were discussed, changed, and finally submitted to the Indian Parliament for its final decision. It took months, sometimes years, of preparation and debate before a program was accepted. The first Five Year Plan was adopted in 1951.

This plan, with $7 billion to spend, concentrated more than a third of the money on increasing food production and building irrigation projects. A Community Development Program was designed to educate and persuade Indian farmers to improve their farming methods. As a result, food production increased by some 4 million tons and the program was declared a success.

The second Five Year Plan (1956–1961) spent almost $14 billion, most of it on developing industries and electric power. Food production increased again under the second plan, but at a lower rate than under the first.

The third plan (1961–1966), involving almost $22 billion, was to raise national income, increase grain production, speed industrial growth, and build power projects. Wars with China (1963) and with Pakistan (1965), however, interfered with this plan, because more money was needed for defense.

A technician demonstrates a solar grain dryer, which is designed to increase India's grain storage capacity.

The fourth plan (1966–1971) and the fifth plan (1971–1975) were quite successful. The next plan, originally scheduled for 1975–1979, was terminated by the state of emergency proclaimed by Indira Gandhi. The sixth and seventh plans took place in 1980–1985 and 1985–1990. The government provided from 40 to 70 percent of the money to carry out these plans. The remainder came from foreign loans and investments. Taxes were raised repeatedly, but they have not produced the money needed to finance the government programs. An income tax is levied on all nonfarming incomes over $400 a year for single persons and $700 for couples. While there is no income tax on agricultural income, there is a heavy land tax.

The accomplishments of economic planning in agriculture have been impressive. Agricultural production has risen, as these figures show:

Year	Food Grains (millions of tons)	Cotton (millions of bales)	Sugar Cane (millions of tons)
1950–1951	50.0	2.9	5.6
1977–1978	125.4	7.1	18.6
1989–1990	170.6	11.4	22.6

The improvement in India's agriculture, to the extent that the country now exports more food than it imports, has been so great that it often is referred to as the "Green Revolution."

The government has always tried to increase agricultural production by gaining the voluntary cooperation of the farmers. Among the programs begun during the 1950s were community development, land reform, irrigation projects, and establishment of cooperatives. They were continued during the 1960s and 1970s and have been the basis for further advances in recent years.

Community Development Programs. In trying to raise agricultural production, the Indian government has tried to gain the voluntary cooperation of farmers. Such cooperation is the main aim of a great educational program known as **Community Development**. It began on October 2, 1952, the 83rd anniversary of Mohandas Gandhi's birth. Beginning with 25,000 villages, most of India's 500,000 villages have been drawn into the program.

Rural India was divided into more than 5,000 blocks. Each consisted of about 100 villages with an area of 150 to 200 square miles and a population of from 60,000 to 70,000. Each block was run by a specially trained block officer, or *gram sevak*, assisted by advisors on agriculture,

121

On a fish farm in India, above, a U.S. advisor works
with a farmer on fish-harvesting techniques.
Experiments with this and with other methods of scientific farming, below, have greatly increased India's
agricultural productivity.

public health, rural industries, animal care, and cooperatives. The block officer's job was to convince villagers to adopt newer methods.

In 1957, a democratic reform was introduced whereby each village elected a *panchayat*, or council. From this council, a representative was elected to the block *panchayat*. The government provided advice, materials, and money. The *panchayat* decided what changes should be introduced. This democratic planning on the village level was an effort to revolutionize Indian agriculture and thereby improve the Indian farmers' way of living.

The Community Development program worked to dig new wells to provide clean water, to construct thousands of miles of new roads, and to improve old roads, thus providing better transportation and ending the isolation that was so long a feature of farm life. Tools and materials were distributed. A new, hopeful attitude gradually developed among the farmers of rural India.

Land Reform.   At the time of independence, much farmland was held by a small number of absentee landlords, large landholders, and *zamindars*, former tax collectors to whom the British had given ownership of the land on which they collected taxes. As many as 25 percent of the Indian farmers did not own any land at all. Others owned small farms, while still others were tenants. This system of landholding was a serious obstacle to agricultural improvement.

In 1953, the central government deprived the *zamindars* of their land and paid them over $1 billion for their holdings. This land was distributed among the farmers, who now pay taxes to the government instead of the rent they formerly paid to the landlords. However, the government could not reform the landholding system further because it did not have the money.

In the 1970s the government decided to limit the average family's landholdings to between four and seven hectares (a hectare is about two and a half acres) when the land was irrigated and produced two crops a year. The limits were 11 hectares if the land was irrigated but produced only one crop per year, and 22 hectares for all other categories of land. The average family consisted of a husband, wife, and three children. It was possible for larger families to obtain more land, up to a maximum of two times the limit. The average size of farms is 2.63 hectares.

Irrigation Projects.   During the 1970s, the central and state governments placed a high priority on increasing irrigation, multiple cropping, fertilizer use, and high-yielding seed varieties in order to improve the

123

productivity of the land. In addition, credit was granted to the farmers and educational information disseminated through extension services. India has slowly reduced its dependence on the monsoons.

Two crops a year can be raised in most areas if water is available during the dry season. For this reason, irrigation is vital in the efforts to increase food production. When India gained its independence, there were 50 million acres of land under irrigation, more than in any other country in the world. Since then, the government has built other irrigation projects to bring more and more land under cultivation. Each of the economic plans has included provisions for this program.

One of the most spectacular is the Bhakra Nangal project on the Sutlej River in the Punjab, in northwestern India. Its 740-foot-high dam, one of the highest in the world, and its 652 miles of canals irrigate 5 to 6 million acres of land.

A farmer in West Bengal plows a field irrigated by a UN-sponsored irrigation and flood control program. The same dam that controls the flow of water also provides the electricity carried by the power lines in the background.

The Thar Desert, some 80,000 square miles of arid land, is to be irrigated by the construction of dams. Trees will be planted and crops suited to arid soil, such as millet, will be raised.

Ten years after independence, some 20 million acres had been brought under irrigation. Local irrigation programs include the improvement of field wells, the digging of deep wells to 200 feet or more, and the use of gasoline engines instead of oxen to bring up water. Over 4,000 such wells have been built in India in recent years.

Farmer indifference or opposition to the new projects is gradually being overcome. In northern India, farmers have increased the use of diesel or electric pumps to bring up water for their lands. It is much cheaper than the old *charsia*, or waterwheel, driven by yoked oxen or bullocks, which raised or lowered water slowly and painfully. In other parts of India, the farmers are slower to adopt these or other simpler irrigation techniques or to use new varieties of seed. However, progress is reported.

Establishment of Cooperatives. To establish larger farms on which better tools and improved techniques can more easily be used, the government has actively promoted the formation of cooperatives. It has persuaded individual farmers to combine their small holdings and has given them much help if they do so. Over 200,000 of these cooperatives were established in the early 1960s. The government provides credit, fertilizer, marketing assistance, storage facilities, and other help to the members. They are often run by officials who are paid by the government. This practice brings the cooperatives more closely under government supervision.

Attempts to form collective farms through the pooling of land for joint cultivation are meeting with much resistance from farmers, who feel deeply about their own plots of ground, small though they may be.

Food Problems. Before the 1970s, India's food needs far exceeded agricultural production every year, so the government had to import food to feed its ever-growing population. Although the United States and the Soviet Union provided millions of tons of wheat and other grains on an annual basis, and other nations have stepped up their aid with food products, malnutrition and famine were major obstacles to India's growth.

Drought and subsequent famine plagued India periodically in the 1960s and 1970s. The United States sent some 10 million tons of wheat in 1966–1967. With additional help from other countries, starvation was

125

averted. Since that time, the concentrated efforts of the government to introduce new strains of rice and wheat, together with increased use of chemical fertilizers and improved irrigation techniques, increased the grain crop of India. More fertilizers have been imported and produced domestically.

POPULATION GROWTH

Some experts argue that India's greatest problem is its population. The ever-growing Indian population has increased overcrowding and food needs, and magnified the shortcomings in housing, health services, and education.

Every year India adds more than 13 million people to its population —people who need places to live, food to eat, and work to do. This is like saying that a city twice as big as New York City is added to India every year. Since independence the population of India has grown by 440 million people. That is more than the individual population of any other country in the world except China.

This rapid increase of population has been due mainly to successful public health measures. Better medical facilities have decreased infant deaths. Epidemics, such as malaria and smallpox, have been controlled. The great increase in population makes the problem of economic development even harder. It makes maintaining the present standard of living difficult.

Most Indians are not opposed to family planning, but children, particularly boys, are greatly desired by Hindus. Such attitudes are slow to change. The government is conducting extensive publicity campaigns for birth control. Clinics where information may be secured are maintained, and birth control devices are distributed free of charge.

However, the government announced in early 1976 that after 24 years, only 17.5 million couples of a total of 103 million in the reproductive ages of 15 to 45 years use contraceptive devices. As a result, cities have announced plans to penalize government employees and residents who do not limit their families to two children. A plan under effect in New Delhi provided incentives to couples with one sterilized spouse or with one who has signed a pledge to undergo sterilization after having two children. Penalties curtailed a couple's access to almost all government assistance, from government jobs and housing to loans, medical care, schools, and even drinking water. Some states even fined and imprisoned couples who failed to comply.

Recently, the Indian government has altered its position on birth control and family planning. Voluntary family planning is now stressed. However, for the foreseeable future India will remain seriously overpopulated.

INDUSTRIAL GROWTH

Before independence, British industries were turning out consumer products such as cement, rubber, leather, glass, and paper. Coal mines, steel plants, cotton mills, and jute mills were in operation. Under the impetus of World War II, there was greater expansion. New industries produced chemicals, bicycles, sewing machines, diesel engines, and machine tools. Shipbuilding and aircraft plants were built.

Expansion of Industry. Since the war there has been considerable expansion of existing industries and the development of new ones. Automobiles, locomotives, electronic equipment, radios, rayon, razor blades, air conditioners, and fertilizers, in addition to machines and machine tools, are now being made.

Under the Five Year Plans, the government devoted increasing amounts of money to speed up industrialization. The large steel con-

An instructor at the Vocational Training Institute in Madras demonstrates welding techniques to a class of trainees.

cern owned by the Tata family was encouraged, with government assistance, to expand its production. New steel plants were built at Raurkela in Orissa (with the help of West Germany), at Durgapur in West Bengal (with British aid), at Bhilai in Madhya Pradesh (with Soviet assistance), and at Bokaro in Bihar. As a result, India is the third largest steel-producing country in Asia, just behind Japan and China. India boasts that it produces steel more cheaply than any other country in the world.

The increase in steel at low cost has greatly stimulated small industry. Plants have been established to make bicycle parts, cardboard boxes, matches, shoes, carpets, preserved foods, and other items. Most employ from ten to 50 workers and use simple machinery. In many instances,

On a street in New Delhi, a vendor sells home-woven decorative rugs called dhurries.

the government helps such companies by giving them electric power at cheap rates, by providing floor space in factories at low rentals, and by paying for the training of workers.

Cottage industry—work done at home, such as spinning and weaving—is still found throughout the country. All the members of a family can work at these ancient industries in their own homes. There are probably more people engaged in earning their livings by cottage industries than in any other kind of economic activity except agriculture. Cottage industries receive government help, particularly in the sale of their products.

India's industrial output has increased dramatically in the last 40 years. However, it should be remembered that India is still basically an agricultural country. Mining and manufacturing account for only one-fifth of the national income of $287 billion. About 6.3 million workers are employed in large and small manufacturing industries, while more than 20 million people are engaged in cottage industries.

Socialism in India. For many years, India called itself a socialist country. Its leading political party, the Congress Party, dedicated itself to government ownership of industry, and its leaders talked of building a socialist society. Actually, private enterprise accounted for 90 percent of the national income, even when the socialist program was at its height.

Under socialism, much of the industry that required large amounts of capital was put into the hands of the government. Some industries were nationalized (taken over by the government). It now owns the railroads, the telephone and telegraph services, the airlines, the life insurance business, the power industry, and the largest banks in the country. It joined with private investors to develop steel production, machine tool manufacturing, and fertilizer processing. However, small factories generally remained as private enterprises. Thus, Indian socialism has been different from the Soviet or Chinese concepts of socialism. In those countries almost all of industry, big and small, was in government hands.

In 1991, the collapse of the Soviet Union and of its socialist economic system led to a rethinking of socialism in India. The government announced that aspects of socialism would be abandoned in favor of a market economy. In particular, some nationalized industries would be returned to private ownership. Foreign investment in India, formerly heavily restricted, would now be welcome, and foreign companies were invited to build factories there.

Welders assemble the body of a dump truck in a factory near Bangalore. India ranks tenth among the world's manufacturing nations.

Financing Industrial Growth.   Raising the money to carry through ambitious programs for industrial and agricultural growth has proved a difficult task for India. Its total annual budget of $56 billion is less than that for California or New York State. Defense expenditures have gone up greatly.

The United States has, since 1951, contributed over $7 billion in gifts and loans, much of it in the form of wheat and rice. Private U.S. foundations, like the Ford and Rockefeller Foundations, have spent over $50 million to improve the health, education, and welfare of the Indian people. U.S. companies have invested over $200 million in Indian industries, mainly oil refining and distribution.

The World Bank and the International Finance Corporation and Development Fund have lent India over $1 billion, mostly for transportation, communications, and power supplies. The USSR lent India more than $1 billion, much of it for steel plant construction. Other countries that have given financial aid—a total of $950 million—include Germany, Britain, Japan, Canada, and France.

Help, or investment, from all these countries must be continued if India is to continue to develop. In 1991 the Indian government introduced policies intended to make investment more attractive to foreign companies. Overseas companies would be allowed a greater degree of control over their businesses in India, and many restrictions on their operations would be done away with.

Water Power.   India's high potential of water power to generate electricity, so important for industry as well as for the consumer, is not yet fully developed. India's power production in a recent year was about 221 million kilowatt hours. Almost two-thirds of this electricity is used by industries, leaving little for the public. The government's irrigation projects have increased hydroelectric power. However, human power and animal power will continue to provide much of the energy required in India for years to come.

Summary.   In the past 30 years, India has increased its food grain production fivefold, and doubled its industrial production. The challenge in the 1990s will be in easing the problems of labor unrest, increasing output in the major industrial plants, and providing adequate supplies of energy to both the factory and the farm. Such transportation problems as port congestion and poor road and highway conditions also need to be remedied.

EDUCATION IN INDIA

The Indian constitution declares that all children should have free and compulsory education to the age of 14. Since independence, the leaders of India have made great efforts to reach this goal, but it has not yet been achieved. Today, about 64 percent of the people cannot read or write. The problems that have to be solved before India becomes a fully literate nation are many and serious.

Education in India is supported and controlled by the various states, much as in the United States. The federal government provides money

131

Above, Indian laborers work at digging an irrigation ditch. In large contruction projects, India often relies on large numbers of workers rather than on bulldozers and other expensive machinery. The dam below provides water storage and hydroelectric power, as well as a lake for fishing.

in the form of grants-in-aid to the states and maintains several nationaluniversities. It attempts to coordinate educational programs throughout the country, offering advice and assisting the states with textbooks, teachers, and equipment.

Education Under the British.   Before the British became the rulers of most of India, education was almost entirely religious. There were no schools for the masses. Whether Hindu or Muslim, the children of the rich were instructed by private teachers.

Under British rule, mission schools and colleges were gradually established. The British East India Company contributed money for education, which was based on the English type of schooling, with instruction in the English language. When the famous historian Thomas B. Macaulay was in the employ of the British East India Company, he made English compulsory. Various other governors–general gave money only to colleges that taught in English. In fact, the company ruled that Indians educated in English-type colleges would be given preference in government jobs. For the next hundred years, this idea dominated higher education in India.

Very little was done about elementary and secondary schooling. The few children who did go to the mission schools in various parts of the country did not stay for more than four years. Only a handful of students from the lower classes continued their education through the university.

Elementary Education Today.   There are over 75 million children between the ages of six and eleven in the primary grades. This is more than the number of U.S. children of the same ages in school. In the United States, however, almost every child is in school. In India only two-thirds of the children of primary school age are in school.

Many of the remaining third do not go to school for the simple reason that there is no school in their neighborhood or village. It would be almost impossible to travel to the next village, where there may be a school, because of a lack of transportation, perhaps even of a road. In other cases, parents are too poor to send their children to school, so they keep them at home to help in the work on the farm or around the house. Sometimes even when there is a school there is no teacher available. School teachers are paid low salaries and do not command much respect in the community. Many teachers are unwilling to serve in rural areas, where living conditions often are poor. There are no recreational or home comforts and few opportunities for advancement.

*These two schoolboys wear the uniform of one of India's
many private schools.*

Even today, only a third of the entering class in first grade will continue to go to school after four years. The number of girls who attend school is much lower than that of boys, partly because parents in many rural areas feel that educating girls is a waste of time.

What is taught in these grades? The teacher, largely through the lecture method (for there are seldom enough books to go around), shows children how to read by writing each word on the blackboard and having children repeat it aloud. They then write the word on small slates or in the dust on the floor. In this way they are taught the elements of reading, writing, spelling, and arithmetic.

Mohandas Gandhi recommended a program of basic education for these schools. He favored teaching the home skills and crafts—cooking, spinning, weaving, and carpentry—in addition to the basic subjects. In this way, he believed, children would be taught to take their places as productive members of the community. To help make the school a little self-supporting, textbooks, notebooks, and other materials could be purchased from the sale of the products made by the children. The government sends teachers from its Community Development program to carry out this Basic Education program, which has been adopted in many schools.

Secondary Education.　There are more than 75,000 secondary schools, with an enrollment of about 40 million students. Many of the schools are state-supported. Others are private schools. The number of students in secondary schools has increased 400 percent since 1960.

The course of study in the secondary schools is determined by university entrance examinations. That is, the subjects taught are mainly for the purpose of passing the examinations that will determine entrance to a university. Much of the instruction is in English, and this creates a serious problem for students whose native language is not English. They have to study English in addition to their regional language. Most textbooks are written in English. The regional languages do not have technical terms, particularly in the sciences and mathematics, thus limiting their use in instruction.

The final examinations are another problem. They are made up by teachers other than the classroom instructors. The exams are based on memorization of facts, and grades on these exams are all-important. The work done by students throughout the year does not count. Those students who pass go on to the next grade, or graduate and are accepted into university-level programs. Those students who fail either repeat the subject or drop out of school. Almost half of the students fail their school finals.

University Education.　In spite of the difficulty of the entrance examination, there has been a great increase in the number of students at the universities. In 1947 there were 200,000 students. There are now over 4 million students in 144 universities and about 800 colleges. All of these, except for nine national universities, are under state control.

The language problem continues to be serious in the universities. Most courses are taught in English. Less than a quarter of the universities offer courses taught in Hindi or one of the regional languages.

CASE STUDY:
The Exam

The following excerpt expresses the author's point of view regarding the aim of education in India—the all-important Exam.

> The Exam is the end-all of Indian schooling. Coming after ten years in some places, eleven years in others, it shapes all the days, all the minutes, in the schoolroom from Class One onward. It is state-administered, something like the Regents exam in New York. But . . . the graduation examination in India includes all the work the children have covered in all their school years.
>
> Though The Exam is the same throughout each state, the style of education varies greatly from the one-room village primary school to the multi-story, high-tuition education factories filled with the children of the rich in Delhi, Bombay, Madras and Calcutta.
>
> Rich urban private-school student and destitute villager, both spend final days of preparation pacing their rooms memorizing "correct" answers, which appear in the published texts of old exams. All questions are essay style and all answers are lengthy. An examinee therefore crams his head with hundreds of thousands of words in the hope that enough of the questions whose answers he has memorized will appear on The Exam to give him a passing mark. Rote is the ideal; original thought is frowned upon. Who knows whether the examiner will recognize an original correct answer as being correct?
>
> Passing marks on The Exam qualify the student to enroll in the university. There he meets a system identical to the one he has just left. Again he must make an irrevocable commitment to a certain subject. . . . And again over all his work looms the specter of the examination he must pass to win his B.A. degree.

Beth Roy, *Bullock Carts and Motor Bikes: Ancient India on a New Road.* New York: Atheneum, 1972, pages 143–147.

1. Why is The Exam more important to Indian youth than other evaluations of their education?

2. According to the author, what effect does the educational system have on Indians? Do you agree? Why or why not?

3. How would you change the educational system in India?

Students at Hindu University in Benares walk toward the Shiva Temple on the university's grounds.

Many of the students who enter the university are not well trained in English. It is difficult for them to use the English textbooks or to understand the professors' lectures in English. With examinations the determining factor in a student's grade, the emphasis is on memorization rather than individual creative work. The low pay does not attract the best qualified professors.

The curriculum of the universities is mainly oriented toward the liberal arts. The humanities courses, such as literature, Greek and Latin, Western history, and art, attract almost 70 percent of the students. Yet India's great need is for trained engineers, scientists, doctors, and technologists. Thousands of students want a college degree for the sake of the degree itself and not because of the type of training involved. Many are unwilling to take a science course because of possible failure, so they take what they think is an easier course, the humanities. To use the university to train for a career runs counter to the traditional Indian belief that learning is an end in itself and should not be related to the mere earning of a living.

Since independence, the government has been putting greater stress on professional education. Technical colleges and polytechnic institutes have been opened, with an enrollment of over 250,000 students. The number of graduates in engineering and technology has increased greatly over the past 30 years. Fourteen rural universities stress vocational programs that include water-control engineering, scientific farming, and rural sociology.

Adult Education.   There are over 200 million Indian adults who are illiterate. The states, with some assistance from the federal government, have set up over 50,000 adult groups called "social education classes" at which the basic elements of literacy are taught, plus lessons in citizenship, health, sanitation, and training in elementary crafts such as sewing.

Two young women learn to write in a literacy class at a village near Lucknow. The Indian government also provides classes in family planning and health education.

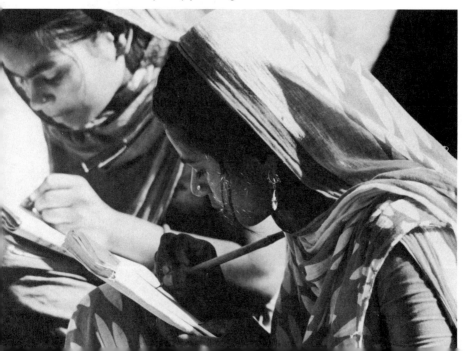

Achievements in Science. The Indian government has developed a chain of more than 25 National Laboratories to conduct high-level research in applied science in a wide variety of fields, from nuclear physics to solar energy. India now ranks fourth in the world in the number of advanced research scientists that it employs. One institute is working on methods to use India's low-grade coal. A food research institute at Mysore is conducting experiments on new food products. In 1968 the Bhabha Atomic Research Center near Bombay was opened.

The role of the intellectual is honored in India. A distinguished scientist, Dr. C. V. Raman, won the Nobel Prize in physics in 1930. Other scientists have won worldwide honors and fame. There are more than 250,000 highly educated people in India today, a figure surpassed in Asian countries only by Japan and China.

The contrast between the illiterate and the intellectual is enormous. The government is making a serious effort to improve the quality of education that is available to most of its people (which is admittedly low) as well as to make it available to even more people.

URBAN LIFE

About 210 million Indian people live in the cities. The rapid rate of growth of cities since independence has been due to the movement of people from the villages. Most of the Indian migrants left their villages because of overpopulation there and a lack of earning opportunities. Sons of farmers could not inherit parts of their fathers' land, already too small to provide a living. So they moved away to the city.

As part of recent Five Year Plans, the Indian government is promoting rural and cottage industrial development to encourage people to remain in the villages. This program is intended to solve some of the unemployment and urban problems in such overcrowded cities as Calcutta.

Of the 11.6 million people who live in metropolitan Calcutta, more than 3 million live in slum dwellings called *bustees*. Thousands of people sleep in the city's streets every night because they have no homes of their own. Unemployment is serious. The crowds of people in the narrow streets make Calcutta a congested city, even though there is a scarcity of buses, cars, and even bicycles.

All the same, there have been remarkable improvements in the life of Calcutta. Government planners have been tearing down the city's slum tenements and building housing projects. Safe drinking water has

The street scene in New Delhi is typical of India's cities.

been provided, and underground sewers, paved streets, lighting, and community bathhouses have been constructed. Work projects to employ thousands are being developed. Although financing these developments has not always been easy, the government has pushed ahead with them. Cholera, a disease caused by poor sanitation and formerly the cause of many deaths, has been eliminated from the city. Similar improvements have been made in other cities.

Air pollution is severe in many of India's cities. In Agra, it threatens damage to the Taj Mahal, India's greatest architectural treasure. The worst incident—in fact, the worst industrial accident of all time, anywhere—occurred in 1984, when a gas leak at a Union Carbide chemical plant in the city of Bhopal killed at least 1,500 people and injured tens of thousands of others.

THE ARTS OF INDIA

From ancient times, almost all forms of classical art have been bound up in the spiritual life for the Hindu people. Architecture, music, drama, painting—all reflect people's efforts to achieve union with God. The Mogul rulers introduced their own tradition with their beautiful mosques and tombs. They also introduced an art that portrayed animals, birds, and the court and country life of contemporary people. The great architectural achievements of this period included the Agra Fort, the Taj Mahal, and the Red Fort at Delhi.

Since independence, modern Indian art has shown considerable growth, with increased variations in styles: some based on old themes, others employing new ideas. The architectural design of the city of Chandigarh (CHUN-dee-gahr), the capital of Punjab, has received world attention. In these buildings, traditional Indian designs are skillfully blended with modern ones.

The Dance. Indian dancing is also largely religious in concept. It was a highly developed art at least 2,000 years ago. There are several important types of Indian dance. They include the Bharata Natyam, Kathakali, and Kathak. Bharata Natyam (BUH-ruhd-uh NAH-tyuhm), the most famous, was born in the temples of the south, and is highly stylized. It takes over ten years to train a dancer accomplished in the traditional gestures and footwork. There are some 140 distinct and recognized poses, and the dancer must show a remarkable control over his or her muscles, particularly those of the face, neck, and hands.

Kathakali (kahd-uh-KAH-lee) is an ancient dance-drama of South India that is characterized by elaborate makeup, rich costumes, and fantastic headdresses. The brilliantly dressed dancers take their themes from the great Indian epics. They use mime, which employs subtle facial expressions and elaborate hand movements.

The third dance type, called Kathak (kuh-TAHK), is found largely in northern India. It interprets short episodes from the early life of Krishna and also the everyday life of the people. It features lightning footwork and requires an excellent sense of rhythm.

There is also a wealth of material in the folk dances of India. The most famous is Manipuri (man-uh-POOR-ee), for which beautiful and distinctive clothes are worn. Whatever the form of dancing, the art of pantomime, which is without sound, is highly developed. The dancer is, essentially, a story teller. Each gesture of eye or eyebrow, hand or finger, neck or foot has its traditional meaning.

The graceful bearing of
the Indian dancer, left,
shows the delicate arm
and hand positions
that are central to the
classical dance forms
of India. Below, a
scene from the film
Two Daughters by the
great Bengali filmmak-
er Satyajit Ray.

Music. Indian music is not easy for an American to understand or appreciate. It is essentially melodic, not harmonic, and is based on a highly elaborate system of notes and melodies. Each piece of music consists of a particular arrangement of notes, called a raga (RAH-gah), of which there are over 70,000, and is intended to portray a particular emotion or feeling or create the flavor of a particular season or time. The music is played on stringed instruments, such as the tambura (tam-BOOR-uh) and sitar (suh-TAHR); on wind instruments, including flutes; and percussion instruments, such as various kinds of drums.

Film. India produces a greater number of movies each year than any other country in the world. Most of them are romantic love stories, which have a special appeal in a country where, even today, most marriages are arranged by parents. Kissing is never shown, however, as most Indians consider it improper to show kissing in public.

Indian movies appeal mainly to Indian audiences and are seldom seen in other countries. However, the films of Satyajit Ray, a Bengali director from Calcutta, are exceptions to this rule. Ray is admired worldwide, particularly for his set of three films called *The World of Apu*. In 1992, a few weeks before Ray's death, the U.S. film industry presented him with a special Academy Award for his life's work.

Indian culture, as expressed through its art, music, and dance, continues to reflect age-old traditions and customs, even under the impact of 20th-century European influences.

THE ROLE OF WOMEN IN INDIA

When the Muslims conquered and ruled a large part of India, they introduced the custom of *purdah*, the seclusion of women and the covering of their faces in the company of all men except their immediate family. Other practices developed that indicated the inferior position of women, such as child marriages and polygamy.

Under British Rule. The British permitted the personal laws of the various religious groups and castes to prevail in matters of marriage, inheritance of property, and family relations. In northern villages, even today, women keep out of sight when men are present.

Under Mohandas Gandhi's leadership, women were encouraged to take an active part in his civil-disobedience campaigns. They picketed shops, prepared and distributed literature, and served as messengers.

143

Some of the Indian states permitted women to vote, provided they met property and educational requirements. Few women could qualify. The Constitution of 1950 granted the right to vote to all adult men and women without property or educational requirements.

Since Independence. Although religious opposition from orthodox Hindus was strong, Nehru was able to have laws adopted that changed the legal and social status of women. Polygamy is prohibited by law, and divorce is now recognized. Minimum ages for marriage were set at 15 for females and 18 for males. The rights of women to adopt children, to inherit property, to buy and sell, and otherwise to engage in activities closed before to them, have also been made into law.

New careers are opening for the modern woman. Medicine is one, politics another, teaching a third. However, the ancient traditions that emphasize a wife's submission, obedience, devotion, and dedication to her husband's every wish still bind the Hindu woman, in spite of her legal emancipation.

There have been some outstanding women in public life. For many years Nehru's daughter, Indira Gandhi, was Prime Minister of India. Nehru's sister, Vijaya Lakshmi Pandit (vee-JAH-yah LAHK-shmee PAHN-dit), served as Indian Ambassador to Moscow and to Washington. In 1953 and 1954 she was President of the United Nations General Assembly, the first woman chosen to fill this office. Some universities have women chancellors, and many colleges have women principals. India has a higher percentage of women doctors than does the United States, and there are a far greater number of women in its national and state legislatures.

Such women are exceptions, however. The vast majority of women are far less educated than men. As in most countries, emancipation has not yet brought equality to Indian women.

REVIEWING THE CHAPTER

I. Building Your Vocabulary

In your notebook, write the correct term that matches the definition.

raga	Five Year Plan	cottage industry
panchayat	*zamindar*	Green Revolution

1. a former tax collector who became a landlord under British rule

2. a form of Indian music

3. a highly planned economic program directed by the government

4. handicrafts of many kinds, including spinning and weaving

5. village council

6. increase in India's output of wheat and rice, due to the use of new types of grains, more fertilizer, and improved irrigation

II. Understanding the Facts

In your notebook, write the numbers from 1 to 5. Write the letter of the correct answer to each question next to its number.

1. Which of the following limits India's industrial development?
   a. lack of natural resources
   b. unwillingness of the government to support industrialization
   c. insufficient capital

2. Which is the most important single occupation of the Indian people?
   a. factory work   b. trade and commerce   c. farming

3. How is the course of study in India's secondary schools determined?
   a. by the individual teacher
   b. by university entrance examinations
   c. by the national department of education

4. Which of the following does the government of India own and operate?
a. all the nation's industries
b. the railroads and airlines
c. factories making cotton cloth and automobiles

5. Why do many Indians leave rural villages for city life?
a. They believe there are more jobs in the cities.
b. The cities offer better housing and comforts.
c. There is no future in the villages.

III. Thinking It Through

In your notebook, write the numbers from 1 to 5. Write the letter of the correct conclusion to each sentence next to its number.

1. Each of the following statements describes a reason for a serious food problem in India *except*:
a. India's farms tend to be very large.
b. India's farms tend to be very small.
c. Indian farmers use primitive tools.
d. Indian farms are not highly productive.

2. A result of the Green Revolution is that:
a. despite some notable improvements in agriculture, India is still unable to feed its people.
b. on most farms, the absentee landlord takes most of the crops.
c. India now exports more food than it imports.
d. the government holds grain in reserve for bad monsoon years.

3. India needs irrigation systems for each of the following goals *except*:
a. to reduce its dependence on the monsoons.
b. to enable farmers in most areas to produce two crops a year.
c. to allow farmers to cultivate the Thar Desert.
d. to reduce population growth.

4. India has been a socialist country because:
a. the nation's laws forbid any private enterprise.
b. the government owns all of India's factories.
c. the government owns much of the industry that requires large amounts of capital.
d. the government owns all the land that can be used for producing crops.

5. Indian college students are more likely to study the humanities than the sciences because:

a. they are afraid of failing in difficult science courses.

b. the highest paying jobs in India go to graduates in the humanities.

c. there is little need for experts in science in India.

d. Indians were not allowed to study the humanities under the British.

DEVELOPING CRITICAL THINKING SKILLS

1. Give evidence that India has a high potential for industrial development.

2. What is the apparent contradiction between India's economic potential and its economic reality?

3. Explain why new farming methods such as new seed or new tools can upset village life.

4. Explain why obtaining capital is a major problem for the Indian economy.

5. Give one argument for and one argument against government control of large industry in India.

6. Assess the position of women in India.

INTERPRETING A GRAPH

Study the graph on page 148 and answer the questions that follow. Write the answers in your notebook.

1. What is external trade?

2. Did India's exports balance its imports in any of the years shown?

3. In which year did the amount of India's imports most exceed the amount of exports?

4. How can you find the value of the imports and exports in American dollars?

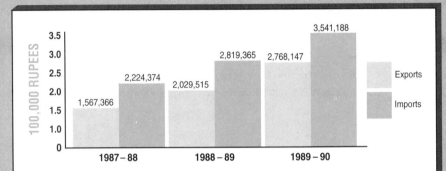

INDIA'S EXPORTS AND IMPORTS
Value in 100,000 rupees for the year ended March 31, 1989

EXPORTS	VALUE	IMPORTS	VALUE
Meat and meat preparations	9,447	Wheat	37,816
Marine products	63,250	Rice	19,346
Processed foods		Raw wool	15,753
(miscellaneous)	12,112	Pulp and waste paper	25,280
Rice	33,147	Crude rubber, including synthetic	
Vegetables and fruits	44,160	and reclaimed	17,264
Coffee and coffee		Synthetic and regenerated fiber	3,743
substitutes	27,971	Fertilizers, crude	18,509
Tea and maté	59,896	Sulphur and unroasted iron	
Spices	25,080	pyrites	24,959
Oilcake	37,043	Metalliferous ores and metal	
Tobacco unmanufactured		scrap	67,742
and tobacco refuse	10,293	Petroleum, petroleum products,	
Raw cotton	2,802	and related materials	437,404
Iron ore	67,250	Edible oil	72,701
Ores and mineral		Organic chemicals	112,701
(excluding mica, iron,		Inorganic chemicals	81,283
and coal)	31,330	Medical and pharmaceutical	
Cotton yarn, fabrics, and		products	20,209
madeup articles	113,130	Fertilizers, manufactured	49,295
Readymade garments	209,753	Artificial resins, plastic	
Jute manufactures,		materials, etc.	81,014
including twist and yarn	24,991	Chemical materials and products	20,409
Leather and leather		Paper, paper board, and	
manufactures	148,950	manufactures thereof	30,570
Natural silk textiles	18,588	Textile yarn, fabrics, and	
Man-made textiles	17,095	madeup articles	28,734
Carpets, mill made	9,171	Pearls, precious and semi-	
Plastic and manufactures		precious stones	317,521
thereof	9,710	Nonmetallic mineral manufactures	16,583
Sports goods	7,881	Iron and steel	193,726
Gems and jewelry	439,899	Nonferrous metal	78,582
Works of art	32,562	Manufactures of metal	19,385
Handmade carpets	46,956	Machinery other than electric	437,090
Engineering goods	232,166	Electrical machinery	160,802
Petroleum products	50,496	Transport equipment	76,666
Chemicals and allied		Professional, scientific, controlling	
products	143,691	instruments, photographic,	
		optical, watches and clocks	69,574

Source: Statesman's Yearbook, 1991–1992

INTERPRETING A CHART

Study the chart on page 148 and answer the questions that follow. Write the answers in your notebook.

1. What were India's three most valuable categories of exports?

2. What were India's three most valuable categories of imports?

3. To what use does India put the pearls, precious stones, and semi-precious stones that it imports?

4. What was the total value of the foodstuffs imported by Indians?

5. What was the total value of India's exports of textiles and jute, including manufactured and raw materials?

6. Find two items that India both exported and imported. Speculate about why this might happen.

ENRICHMENT AND EXPLORATION

1. Prepare a short report on environmental problems and pollution in India, including the problem of the silting and salting in irrigation canals.

2. Read Kusum Nair's *Blossoms in the Dust* and report on ways that traditional social and religious values conflict with economic progress.

3. Listen to some of the music of Ravi Shankar or Ali Akbar Khan on record, cassette tape, or CD. Make a report to the class about Indian music, and play a short example for the class.

4. The motion picture industry in India is the world's largest. Using the *Reader's Guide to Periodical Literature* and the card catalog, find material about the Indian movies. Write a report about the kinds of films made in India and their stars.

5. In some way the Green Revolution has had an adverse effect on the position of rural Indian women. Do research on this problem and decide what measures, if any, can be taken to counter the negative effects.

INDIA AND THE WORLD
1950–Today

1950–1953	*Korean War*
1951–1956	India's first Five Year Plan
1952	Community Development program begins.
1953	Government takes *zamindar* land as part of land reform.
1954	French withdraw from enclaves in India.
	Pancha Shila agreement with China
1957	India incorporates its territory in Kashmir.
1959	*Tibetans rebel against Chinese.*
1960	Indus River Agreement with Pakistan
1961	*Berlin Wall is built.*
	India seizes Goa and other Portuguese possessions in India.
1962	China invades India.
1963	Pakistan and China agree on borders.
1964–1972	*Vietnam War*
1965–1966	War between India and Pakistan
1968	India opens atomic research center.
1971	East Pakistan becomes independent Bangladesh with military help from India.
	India and USSR sign friendship treaty.
1975	USSR launches India-built satellite.
1976	India and Pakistan resume diplomatic relations.
1984	Gas leak at Bhopal kills 1,500 people.
1991	India announces greater emphasis on a market economy, less on socialism.
	Soviet Union collapses.

7 India in the World of Nations

India has often been regarded as the spokesperson for the developing third world nations. In fact, since India became independent, it has played a major role in international as well as Asian affairs. India's size and large population alone make its voice strong and significant. Its resources and industrial progress make India the second leading industrialized nation in Asia. And the peaceful way in which India secured its freedom, led by such figures as Mohandas Gandhi and Jawaharlal Nehru, became a model for other countries under foreign control.

POLICY OF NONALIGNMENT

India called its basic foreign policy "nonalignment." Many leaders of the Western world labeled this policy as "neutrality." Nehru denied this bitterly. A neutral country, he said, will not intervene on either side of a dispute, no matter what the cause. Under "nonalignment," a nation does not commit itself in advance to support the policies of another country. Instead, it decides each question involving other countries on its own merits, and reserves freedom to take what steps it feels will help resolve the conflict. He argued that such a policy would check the growing division of the world into two opposing camps. It would limit possible violence by enabling India to serve as a mediator, one with no axe of its own to grind, and thus help the cause of peace. This policy became popular with many of the new, small and weak nations that were reluctant to choose sides in the Cold War. India became their leader.

The nonalignment policy of Nehru was not understood by many U.S. citizens. They could not grasp the seemingly contradictory Indian policies of accepting economic aid from the United States, yet opposing many measures favored by the United States. India persistently voted for the People's Republic of China's admission to the United Nations, a policy opposed by the United States for many years. It also refused to support U.S. resolutions condemning Soviet invasions of Hungary and Czechoslovakia. Even as Nehru condemned the use of aggression, India seized the Portuguese enclave of Goa. An **enclave** is a country or part of country lying wholly within the boundaries of another nation.

FOREIGN COLONIES IN INDIA

When Britain granted independence to India in 1947, France and Portugal still retained small holdings—a few ports and trading posts on the subcontinent. Nehru called these "pimples on the face of India." They were constant reminders of Western imperialism. To free these enclaves seemed to be necessary if the Indians were to eliminate all evidences of Western control.

The French in India. Even though the French had been defeated by the British in their efforts to expand their control over India (see page 75), they continued to hold the ports of Pondichéry, Chandernagor, and several others. This French territory amounted to less than 200 square miles, with a population of some 350,000. In 1954, France voluntarily withdrew.

The Portuguese in India. The Portuguese were not so obliging. They held three slices—Goa, Damão, and Diu—on the west coast, and they had been there for over 450 years. They regarded these territories as "overseas provinces" of Portugal and refused to withdraw. Although Nehru insisted that Goa must become part of India, he was opposed to the use of force to take it.

But suddenly, in December 1961, the Indian army invaded Goa and took it over. In spite of United States and United Nations efforts to prevent this use of force, the Indian government occupied the other Portuguese possessions and thus eliminated the last foreign holdings in the country.

RELATIONS WITH PAKISTAN

Partition of India in 1947 into the two states of Islamic Pakistan and Hindu India intensified many old problems and created new ones. What had been political, religious, and economic rivalries between two groups of people in the same country became international incidents involving two independent states. Even the division of money, factory and office equipment, railroad cars, and river waters became international problems. The rioting and killing that accompanied the mass migrations of Hindus and Muslims from one state to the other made the already bad feelings worse.

The Indus River System Problem. The Indus River flows through Pakistan. During British occupation, an extensive system of irrigation canals had been built to provide the necessary water for the farmlands there. However, the beginning of the Indus River is in India. When Pakistan became independent, the Islamic government was afraid that India would divert the waters of the Indus River and some of its tributaries for its own use, thus turning much of Pakistan's irrigated land into desert.

This problem was taken up by the International Bank for Reconstruction and Development (or World Bank), an agency of the United Nations, which secured an agreement in 1960 that was satisfactory to both countries. Under this agreement, the waters of three western rivers (the Indus, the Jhelum, and the Chenab) are reserved for Pakistan's use, and the waters of three eastern rivers (the Ravi, the Beas, and the Sutlej) for Indian use. Since two thirds of the irrigated area and 40 million Pakistanis (as against 10 million Indians) are dependent on these rivers for irrigation, the division gave Pakistan the greater amount of water.

New dams, reservoirs, and irrigation works are being constructed by both countries to increase by 30 million acres the cultivated areas in the northwest. This billion-dollar program is being helped by contributions from the United States, the World Bank, and other countries.

Kashmir. Kashmir, in northwestern India, was one of the largest princely states before partition. Its population of over 5 million lived in an area of 86,000 square miles. The ruler of Kashmir was a Hindu maharajah, but about three fourths of the population were Muslims. When India was divided in 1947, the maharajah was given the choice of joining with either Pakistan or India.

While he was deciding, Muslims from Pakistan invaded Kashmir. This move persuaded the Hindu ruler to join India. Indian troops were quickly sent into Kashmir. Pakistan also sent in its soldiers. India appealed to the United Nations, which succeeded, after a year of fight-

The beautiful and seemingly peaceful Vale of Kashmir has been a cause of friction between India and Pakistan since the 1940s.

ing, in arranging a cease-fire in January 1949. The western and northern parts of the disputed territory (about one third of its total area) were in Pakistani hands. The remaining two thirds were under Indian control.

Under the cease-fire agreement, a plebiscite (a vote on a question) was to allow the people of Kashmir to choose for themselves which country they wanted to join. The United Nations was to hold this plebiscite. This has never been done, in spite of United Nations efforts to secure Pakistani-Indian cooperation.

The Indian government introduced economic and social reforms in the part of Kashmir it held, in an effort to persuade the people to become part of India. In 1957 India incorporated its Kashmir territory. Pakistan objected and tried again to get the United Nations to hold the promised plebiscite.

In 1962, China attacked India and took over some 12,000 square miles of Indian territory. In 1963, Pakistan reached an agreement with China regarding the borders of Pakistani-held Kashmir. The drawing together of Pakistan and China caused India many misgivings. Relations between Pakistan and India grew worse.

Border violation charges increased between India and Pakistan in 1965. Sharp fighting broke out near the southern Pakistani-Indian border. This was halted by a cease-fire within a month. In September 1965, a full-fledged war involving planes, tanks, and soldiers broke out between the two countries, as each invaded the other's territory. For three weeks, this undeclared war went on. Then the United Nations Security Council succeeded in securing a cease-fire agreement.

In January 1966, the Soviet Union brought together the leaders of the two countries, Shastri of India and Ayub Khan of Pakistan. They met at Tashkent, Uzbekistan, in the Soviet Union. At this conference, the two countries agreed to withdraw their soldiers to positions held before the fighting.

After the Indian-Pakistani war in 1971, which resulted in the creation of an independent Bangladesh from the former state of East Pakistan (see Chapter 8), new meetings were held on the Kashmir issue. In July 1972, Pakistani President Ali Bhutto and Indian Prime Minister Indira Gandhi signed a peace treaty. Later, a joint statement was issued laying down guidelines for demarcation of the disputed Kashmir border and promising that it would be "respected by both sides without prejudice to the recognized positions of either side."

Although Kashmir remained divided, India and Pakistan resumed diplomatic and economic ties. In November 1974, the two governments signed a treaty reestablishing trade relations. Diplomatic ties as well as air and rail service were resumed in July 1976. The two nations continue to assess each other's moves cautiously, especially nuclear weapon research and defense spending and development.

Bangladeshi guerrillas ride an Indian tank toward Dhaka in December 1971, a few days before the end of the war that brought independence to Bangladesh.

After 1988, a new movement for the independence of Kashmir troubled both India and Pakistan. India, however, fears that making Kashmir independent would lead to similar demands from other Indian states. Pakistan also is opposed to an independent Kashmir, since Pakistan's position as the homeland for all Muslims on the subcontinent would be undermined by an independent Islamic state on its doorstep.

RELATIONS WITH THE SOVIET UNION

India's foreign policy was based on nonalignment, intended to encourage friendly and peaceful relations among all nations. At the same time, government officials built a close relationship with the Soviet Union. After 1971, when India and the USSR signed a mutual peace treaty, the two nations enjoyed strong diplomatic ties.

Until the collapse of the Soviet Union in 1991, relations between it and India were good for a number of reasons:

- Geographically the two countries, although not next-door neighbors, were close to each other. Tajikistan, one of the former Soviet republics, is separated from Kashmir by only a thin strip of Afghanistan territory.

- Ideologically, there was much similarity between the two countries. India's efforts to improve its industrial and agricultural output through centrally planned Five Year Plans were similar to the Soviet Union's economic program. Government control of large sectors of the economy was similar in both countries. The early economic progress of the USSR was an inspiration to Indian leaders, who hoped to do for their country what the Soviet leaders seemed to have done for theirs.

- Diplomatically, the two countries were friendly from 1947 onward. Soviet leaders like Khrushchev and Kosygin paid state visits to India, and Indian leaders visited Moscow. The USSR supported India's actions in Goa and Kashmir. The Soviet Union supplied late-model planes when China attacked in 1962, and it offered to build factories in India so that India could make its own planes. It was Soviet diplomacy that brought Indian and Pakistani leaders together at Tashkent in 1966 to agree to withdraw their troops from each other's territory.

*Indian Prime Minister Lal Bahadur Shastri, right, is
greeted by Anastas Mikoyan, a high Soviet official, upon
his arrival in Moscow in 1965. The Soviet Union was one
of the first countries that Shastri visited as Indian leader.*

- Economically, the Soviet Union was of great financial and technical help to India. The USSR lent India more than $1 billion, most
of it going to build oil refineries and steel plants. Soviet technicians
trained Indian workers to operate these new factories. Soviet food
shipments enabled India to overcome wheat shortages. This aid
was widely publicized in India and created a favorable image of the
USSR.

- A 20-year treaty of peace, friendship, and cooperation was signed
between India and the USSR in 1971. The Soviet Union launched
an Indian-built satellite into orbit in 1975, and this event was followed by an official state visit to Moscow by Prime Minister Indira
Gandhi. Good relations continued between the two countries until
the demise of the Soviet Union in 1991.

RELATIONS WITH COMMUNIST CHINA

India's problems with the People's Republic of China in the past rank second only to its difficulties with Pakistan. When China occupied Tibet in 1950, it became India's next-door neighbor. Relations between the two countries were friendly until 1962.

India was one of the strongest supporters of China's admission to the United Nations. Over the years, exchanges of official visits of leaders, agricultural and technical experts, and cultural delegations had brought the two countries close together. Both countries were breaking away from foreign control. Both were pursuing programs to improve the standard of living of their people.

Nehru and Mao Zedong of China, in 1954, agreed on a general statement of principles, which Nehru called the *Pancha Shila*. Its "five principles" included mutual nonaggression, respect for territorial integrity, noninterference in domestic affairs, peaceful coexistence, and equality. These principles were reaffirmed the following year at the Bandung Conference of Afro-Asian nations, to which India had invited China.

Tibetan Revolt. The first major break between China and India took place in 1959, when the people of Tibet rebelled against the Chinese. This rebellion had been building up since the Chinese takeover in 1950. The Dalai Lama, who was both religious and political ruler of the Tibetans, was forced to flee. The Indian people and government welcomed him. Chinese troops thereupon crossed the eastern section of India's long northern border and occupied some Indian territory.

Nehru appealed to China to withdraw the soldiers and live up to the *Pancha Shila* agreement. China countered by charging that the Indian government had encouraged the Tibetans to revolt. It demanded some 50,000 square miles of Indian territory. For the next three years, one country leveled charges against the other.

The Chinese Attack India. Suddenly, in October 1962, Chinese troops crossed the disputed boundary line between Tibet and India and defeated the Indian army stationed there. India appealed to both Britain and the United States for military help. Both countries rushed supplies. The United States sent small arms and ammunition and some transport planes to airlift Indian troops into the battle areas. Although Nehru also asked Russia for help, the Soviet government urged India to accept the Chinese proposal for a cease-fire and delayed any military aid.

Just as quickly as it began, the fighting ended. The Chinese halted their attack and pulled their troops back. However, they kept much of the territory they had won. China still occupies the land that it gained, and it has declared that it is now Chinese territory.

Effects of the Invasion. One major result of this brief but sharp invasion was that India began to build up its armaments and defense positions. This meant that money and materials badly needed for the economic and social development of the country had to be diverted to military purposes.

Many Indians took another look at Nehru's foreign policy of nonalignment. Questions were raised about the country's lack of military preparedness. The invasion created doubts among the neutral nations of the world about India's leadership. Above all, it pointed up the deep rivalry between India and China, with the leadership of Asia hanging in the balance. To what extent would the smaller Asiatic nations and India's small neighbors, Bhutan and Nepal, be able to depend on India in the event of trouble?

Another factor that weakened Indian-Chinese relations was the threat of China as an atomic power. China had joined the atomic club by exploding atomic and hydrogen bombs. India also has the potential to become a nuclear power and continues to devote research and financial resources in the peaceful as well as military applications of atomic energy.

Relations with China continued to deteriorate during the early 1970s, particularly as a result of China's support of Pakistan in the Pakistani civil war that resulted in the formation of Bangladesh. Tensions began to ease in 1976 when the two countries exchanged diplomatic representatives. Two years later, China sent a special trade delegation to India, the first such mission since 1962. In the 1980s, under Rajiv Gandhi, relations between India and China continued to improve.

INDIA AND THE UNITED STATES

The largest democracy in Asia and the largest democracy in the West have not always been the best of friends. Sympathy for Indian hopes of independence had been expressed by many Americans before and during World War II. After freedom had been achieved, the United States supported Indian admission into the United Nations and hoped it would be a model for other new states to follow.

Conflicting U.S. Opinions. The United States has found it somewhat difficult to support some of India's policies. The U.S. government also has tended to regard India as a rather unimportant world power. In 1954, Pakistan joined in a U.S. alliance against the Soviet Union and accepted military aid. This move shook Indian leaders, and relations between India and the United States became cool. Certainly the different geographic locations and different historical and cultural experiences require that patience prevail in working out a good relationship.

The U.S. government has been concerned and confused that in the midst of severe economic difficulties, the Indian government has devoted so much money, time, and resources to the development of a nuclear weapon. The Indian government still maintains its policy of nonalignment, but it claims that its status as a nuclear power will aid in bringing peace and stability to the world.

The ending of the state of emergency in 1977 relieved many Americans who had become concerned with violations of human rights in India under Indira Gandhi. Since the late 1970s, both India and the United States worked, with limited success, to improve relations between the two nations.

The United States provided food and economic assistance to India since its independence. U.S. technical aid enabled India to build factories, train workers, construct dams and irrigation projects, and extend health programs. In addition, various U.S. relief organizations and foundations made large contributions to educational programs.

U.S. economic aid was reduced in 1968. There were major differences between the United States and India on such issues as India's stand against U.S. involvement in Vietnam, India's silent support of the Soviet invasion of Czechoslovakia, and Indian-Soviet arms agreements and defense treaties.

Conflicting Indian Opinions. Indians did not understand why the United States built up Pakistan as a military ally. They regard this as a threat to them, and them only. To Indians, the Southeast Asia Treaty Organization (SEATO) and the Baghdad Pact, anti-Communist alliances that Pakistan joined, were more dangerous to India than to the USSR or China.

When the United States withdrew financial support for the building of a government-owned steel plant, the Indians regarded it as attempted

CASE STUDY:

India's Foreign Policy

In a 1949 speech, Prime Minister Jawaharlal Nehru set forth the basic outline of India's foreign policy. He spoke of his hope that India would be friendly with all nations. He talked of the growing importance of Asia in world affairs and of the need to eliminate racism from the world. Finally, he spoke of what he hoped for in India's relations with Europe and the United States:

> Now, Europe and America, because they have been dominant countries, with a dominant culture, have tended to think that ways of living other than theirs are necessarily inferior. Whether they are inferior or not I do not know. If they are inferior, probably their own people will change them. . . .
>
> The world is a very diverse place, and I personally see no reason why we should regiment it along one line. . . . Perhaps it [this belief] may be due to the whole philosophy of life behind us in India. Whatever we may do in our limited outlook and failings, we have had a type of philosophy which is a live-and-let-live philosophy of life. . . .
>
> With all our failings, we are a very ancient people, and we have gone through thousands and thousands of years of human experience; we have seen much wisdom, and we have seen much folly, and we bear the traces of both that wisdom and that folly around us. We have to learn much. . . ; and perhaps we have to unlearn a great deal too. . . .
>
> I wish all of us would give up the idea of improving others, and improve ourselves instead.

From Jawaharlal Nehru, selected and edited by Dorothy Norman, *Nehru: the First Sixty Years.* Vol. 2. New York: John Day, 1965, pages 470-471.

1. What attitude does Nehru think Europe and the United States sometimes have toward other countries? Does he think that this attitude is justified?

2. What, according to Nehru, explains the outlook of the people of India toward other countries?

3. How does Nehru's last sentence relate to Hinduism? Explain.

interference with their form of government and turned to the Soviets for help. When the United States offered to establish an Indo-American Foundation in India to promote progress in all fields of learning, Indira Gandhi was forced to turn it down because of fear that it would be a cover for spy activities.

The U.S. food aid program, while of tremendous help to the Indian people, was regarded with a great deal of suspicion. It was feared that it would be used to influence government policy toward the United States, especially an attempt to move economic policy more toward capitalism.

Relations since 1970. Relations between the United States and India were seriously damaged by U.S. support of Pakistan in 1971. Tensions eased somewhat in 1973 but flared again when the U.S. government resumed military aid to Pakistan in 1975. The U.S. government also harshly criticized India's suspension of civil liberties and widespread political repression under Prime Minister Gandhi from 1975 to 1977.

Since that time, diplomatic and economic ties have been strengthened. President Carter visited India in 1978. Increased aid for industrial

U.S. President Ronald Reagan, right, listens to Prime Minister Rajiv Gandhi speak at a White House ceremony in 1987. Gandhi's two visits to Washington helped improve relations between India and the United States.

development and health care brought the two nations closer together. Rajiv Gandhi visited the United States twice during the 1980s and was warmly received by both the government and public. India's new economic policy, announced in 1991 (see page 129), seems likely to bring the nations much closer.

INDIA'S NEIGHBORS: NEPAL AND BHUTAN

At the center of India's northern frontier, there is a stretch of about 1,000 miles where India and China are separated by the countries of Nepal and Bhutan.

Nepal. Nepal is the larger of the two states. Its area is about 54,000 square miles, and its population is more than 12 million. It is a constitutional monarchy, ruled by a king. Nepal is a poor country, with more than 90 percent illiteracy. It is important, however, as a stepping stone to the Indian subcontinent. The Nepalese are proud of their independence and have fought to keep it. Their warrior class, the Gurkhas, are excellent soldiers, and many are serving in the Indian army today.

The Buddhist and Hindu religions are practiced in the country. Tribal and caste distinctions are still observed. The lack of transportation and communication lines has hindered the industrial development of this small nation.

India realizes the importance of Nepal and has maintained good relations by a substantial aid program for road building, irrigation projects, drinking water purification, and power projects. The United States also has assisted Nepal, as have Britain, the Soviet Union, and China. Much of this aid has been for the construction of an east-west road to link areas of the country that now can be reached only by traveling through India.

Bhutan. This semi-independent kingdom between India and Tibet has an area of about 18,000 miles and a population of 1.4 million. Although Bhutan has its own king, its defense and foreign relations are directed by India. Bhutan's people are ethnically related to the Tibetans. Buddhism is the dominant religion. In recent years Bhutan has been evolving into a "democratic monarchy" in which the national assembly has veto power over the king.

Three Nepalese on a Himalayan ridge, top, are silhouetted against the clouds. The peak of Annapurna rises 26,504 feet (8,078 meters) in the distance. Above, villagers in Bhutan pass before a combined fortress and monastery that until recently was the capital of the country.

Chapter 7:
CHECKUP

REVIEWING THE CHAPTER

I. Building Your Vocabulary

In your notebook, write the correct term that matches the definition.

nonalignment   Gurkha   enclave
Dalai Lama   plebiscite

1. a member of the warrior class of Nepal

2. a country or part of country lying wholly within the boundaries of another nation

3. a vote to determine the voters' preferred answer to a question

4. policy of not participating in political or military alliances, but deciding each question of foreign policy individually

5. religious leader of the Tibetans

II. Understanding the Facts

In your notebook, write the numbers from 1 to 5. Write the letter of the correct answer to each question next to its number.

1. Which policy began under Nehru's leadership?
   a. alliances with Western nations   b. neutrality
   c. nonalignment

2. What has been the major cause of conflict between Pakistan and India?
   a. the boundaries of Pakistan   b. Kashmir   c. Goa

3. What was decided by the Indus River Agreement?
   a. India received the greater share of waters.
   b. Pakistan received the greater share of waters.
   c. Both countries received equal amounts of the waters.

4. Which nation or group brought about the cease-fire agreement in the 1965 war between India and Pakistan?
a. the United Nations   b. the United States
c. the Soviet Union

5. For what are the Gurkhas best known?
a. literary achievements   b. artistic accomplishments
c. abilities as fighters

III. Thinking It Through

In your notebook, write the numbers from 1 to 5. Write the letter of the correct conclusion to each sentence next to its number.

1. Nehru claimed that India's policy of nonalignment would help stop the world's division into two camps led by
a. the Soviet Union and China.
b. the United States and the Soviet Union.
c. Muslims and those of all other religions.
d. oil-producing nations and importers of oil.

2. India gained control of French enclaves by
a. convincing the French to leave voluntarily.
b. buying the territory from France.
c. invading them and taking them over.
d. refusing to supply the enclaves with food, water, or electricity.

3. The Indus River was a source of conflict between India and Pakistan because
a. Indians complained that Pakistanis deliberately spoiled the river waters for Hindu devotions.
b. Pakistanis feared that Indians would pollute the waters of the Indus.
c. India worried that Pakistan would dam up the river and reduce its flow.
d. Pakistan worried that India would divert the vital waters of the river before they could reach Pakistan.

4. At the time of partition in 1947, Kashmir was ·
a. ruled by a Muslim but had a majority of Hindus in its population.
b. ruled by a Hindu but had a majority of Muslims in its population.
c. ruled by a Hindu with a Hindu majority in the population.
d. ruled by a Muslim with a Muslim majority in the population.

5. Parts of Kashmir are occupied by
   a. India, Pakistan, and China.
   b. Nepal, India, and Pakistan.
   c. India, Pakistan, and Bhutan.
   d. India, Pakistan, and Bangladesh.

DEVELOPING CRITICAL THINKING SKILLS

1. Explain why Indian government officials built a close relationship with the USSR between 1950 and 1991.
2. Why did many Americans misunderstand India's policy of nonalignment during the Cold War?
3. Why did Indians react unfavorably to United States aid to Pakistan?
4. What political and social issues cause conflict in Kashmir?
5. Why are Nepal and Bhutan important to India?

UNDERSTANDING POINTS OF VIEW

Two people may witness the same event and describe it very differently, depending on their point of view. Point of view is influenced by a person's background, politics, religion, education—whatever shapes his or her way of looking at the world. Read the following accounts of the Kashmiri conflict from the Pakistani and Indian points of view. Then answer the questions that follow. Write the answers in your notebook.

View 1: For religious, political, economic, and strategic reasons, Kashmir's voluntary accession to Pakistan was universally considered a foregone conclusion. But to the shock of the Kashmiris, their Hindu ruler—in defiance of the wishes of his people—acceded secretly to India. The Kashmiri people rose in rebellion. The Hindu overlord summoned India's assistance to suppress the revolt. The Indian army moved in . . .

View 2: The United Nations . . . failed to ease the tensions and instead rubbed salt into the wounds of the contestants. . . . The fact that Pakistan had been the aggressor in Kashmir was almost forgotten. . . . India was puzzled by the fact that in the hands of the United Nations the Kashmir issue had turned from a clear case of aggression into a complicated dispute over territorial sovereignty.

View 3: The commitments made by both countries aside, the vital interests of the people of Jammu and Kashmir do not seem to have been heeded sufficiently. Indeed, over these long years they have suffered incalculable harm and pain. The uncertainty to which they have been subjected has eaten into their very vitals, and until it is removed no progress in any sphere . . . can be achieved.

1. Which viewpoint do you think is that of a native of Kashmir? Explain your answer, using words or ideas from the extract.
2. Which viewpoint do you think is that of an Indian? Explain your answer, using words or ideas from the extract.
3. Which viewpoint do you think is that of a Pakistani? Explain your answer, using words or ideas from the extract.
4. Does one of the viewpoints strike you as better than the others? Explain.

INTERPRETING A MAP

Study the map of Kashmir below and answer the questions that follow. Write the answers in your notebook.

1. Which four countries border Kashmir?
2. What river flows through Kashmir?
3. What is capital of Kashmir? Is it controlled by India or by Pakistan?

ENRICHMENT AND EXPLORATION

1. India has been proposed as one of the permanent members of the Security Council in a reorganization of the United Nations. Do research on India's current status within the United Nations.

2. Do research on India's relations with its island neighbor, Sri Lanka. Present your findings to the class in a short report. Be able to locate Sri Lanka on a map.

3. Do research on the customs and cultures of Bhutan. What problems does Bhutan have in trying to maintain its unique culture? The May 1991 issue of *National Geographic* presents an interesting look at the changing world of Bhutan.

4. Write a story for a newspaper on "The Kashmir Dispute." Include in your article the background of the dispute, the efforts at a settlement, and its present status.

5. Using *The New York Times Index* and the *Reader's Guide to Periodical Literature*, research news articles about India's relations with the republics of the former Soviet Union since the Soviet Union's collapse in 1991.

PAKISTAN, BANGLADESH, AND THE WORLD

1947–Today

1945	*World War II ends.*
1947	Pakistan is separated from India, becomes independent.
1948	Death of Muhammad Ali Jinnah
1956	Pakistan adopts new constitution.
1958	Muhammad Ayub Khan takes over Pakistani government.
1960–1963	*John F. Kennedy is U.S. President.*
1969	Yahya Khan takes over Pakistani government.
1970	Cyclone and tidal wave strike East Pakistan.
1971	West Pakistani troops are sent to East Pakistan.
	India sides with East Pakistan in war.
	East Pakistan becomes independent nation of Bangladesh.
1972	Zulfiqar Ali Bhutto becomes prime minister of Pakistan.
1974	Floods cripple Bangladesh.
	Sheik Mujib is named president of Bangladesh.
1975	Sheik Mujib is overthrown and killed.
1977	Muhammad Zia-ul-Haq leads coup in Pakistan.
1978	Ziaur Rahman becomes president of Bangladesh.
1979	Zulfiqar Ali Bhutto is executed.
1980–1990	Civil war in Afghanistan drives millions of refugees into Pakistan.
1981	Rahman dies in unsuccessful coup attempt.
1988	Zia-ul-Haq dies in plane crash.
1988–1990	Benazir Bhutto is prime minister in Pakistan.
1990–1991	*Persian Gulf War*
1991	Tropical storm devastates Bangladesh.

8 Pakistan and Bangladesh

Until 1947, there was no country called Pakistan. Until 1971, there was none called Bangladesh. Since those dates, Pakistan and Bangladesh have been independent nations. These two countries share the history and civilization of India, including its experience under the British. But there are important differences between India and the new nations of Pakistan and Bangladesh.

We have already read about the history of India and the struggle for independence in preceding chapters. In spite of a common historic background, religious differences resulted in the splitting of the subcontinent of India into the separate nations of India and Pakistan. Later, geographic and economic differences brought about the breaking away of Bangladesh from Pakistan.

In this chapter we will examine the history of Pakistan since World War II, including the civil war that led to the independence of Bangladesh.

BACKGROUND TO PAKISTANI INDEPENDENCE

The influence of Islam on the subcontinent of India began in the 8th century, when Arabs from the Middle East first settled in the Indus River region. Several hundred years later, Muslims from Central Asia poured in through the Khyber Pass. The social order of Islam, based on the principle of human equality and universal brotherhood, greatly influenced the caste-dominated Hindu society. By the seventeenth century, almost the entire subcontinent was under the rule of the Mogul Empire. In time, the empire began to fall apart because of internal rivalry and European colonization and domination.

The Mogul Empire ended in 1858, and the struggle for independence from Great Britain began. Under the British, Muslims gradually lost their political power and social prestige. They were overshadowed by the overwhelming Hindu majority and by the colonial policies of the European nations in Asia, particularly the British. The political reawakening of the Muslims began with the efforts of Sir Said Ahmad Khan to revive their political and social rights. The result was the creation of the All-India Muslim League in 1906.

For a time, Muslims cooperated with Hindus in the movement for Indian independence. Two great leaders changed the course of history for India's millions of Muslims. One was Muhammad Iqbal, who through his poetry exalted the Islamic cultural heritage and stressed patriotism. Before his death in 1938, he had popularized the idea of a single, independent Islamic state in India. The man who made this a reality was Muhammad Ali Jinnah.

Muhammad Ali Jinnah. Born in Karachi in 1876, Jinnah received an English education, studied law, entered politics as a supporter of the Indian Congress party, and advocated Hindu-Muslim cooperation. In the 1930s he parted company with the Congress party because he thought it ignored the needs of India's Muslims. He became president of the Muslim League and worked with Muhammad Iqbal for a separate Islamic state, for which he created the name "Pakistan." The name came from the names of several predominantly Islamic states in western India: P (Punjab), A (Afghan Province), K (Kashmir), S (Sind), TAN (Baluchistan). The name is also said to mean "land of the pure," reflecting the spiritual unity of its Islamic inhabitants.

Ali Jinnah's stubborn refusal to accept anything but a separate state for his people left the British no alternative but to yield to his demands. Therefore, when independence was granted to India in 1947, Pakistan was created as a dominion within the British Commonwealth. Ali Jinnah became its governor-general and the president of the Constituent Assembly, created to draw up a constitution for the new state.

The Problems of Partition. Unfortunately for Pakistan, Ali Jinnah died a year later. Liaquat Ali Khan became prime minister. The new leader faced many serious problems caused by the continued bad feelings between India and his country. Among these were the Kashmir question (still unresolved) and control of the major rivers, particularly the Indus, that flow from India into Pakistan. Another was the fact that Pakistan was split into eastern and western segments separated by almost 1,000 miles of India. Perhaps the greatest was the largest migra-

Muhammad Ali Jinnah, the founder of Pakistan, at first worked with Gandhi and Nehru but later became their bitter opponent.

tion of peoples the world has ever known, as Hindus left Pakistan and Muslims left India.

Before this wholesale migration had ended, over 15 million people had moved. About nine million Hindu refugees went to India and some six million Muslims refugees to Pakistan. It is estimated that more than half a million people died on these journeys. There were many disputes over the property the refugees left behind, and the problems of settling and integrating the displaced millions were enormous. The leaders of Pakistan were hindered by a lack of administrative personnel and by the poverty of the country. The major industrial centers and the bulk of administrative machinery had remained in India.

Most of the trained officials in government service, whether in education, finance, or trade, were Indians. The raw materials were raised in the Islamic areas, but the processing factories for jute, the sugar refineries, and the spinning and weaving mills were in Indian hands. Thus, the producing areas were separated from the markets by partition. Even the division between the two countries of the physical assets of the old united country involved serious difficulties. How many locomotives, how much gold, how many typewriters, how much of everything was to go to Pakistan? How much to India? Since India had the greater population, it received the larger share of almost everything. This only increased the bitterness between the two nations.

THE GOVERNMENT OF PAKISTAN

Following the death of Ali Jinnah in 1948, the National Assembly, acting under the amended British Dominion Act of 1935, elected Iskandar Mirza as acting governor-general. However, continued differences between East and West Pakistan delayed the framing of a new constitution. Finally, in early 1956, the differences were sufficiently overcome to permit the drawing up of a new constitution. Mirza was appointed provisional president and a republic was proclaimed.

The adoption of a constitution did not resolve many of the problems facing the new country. Politicians were ambitious and greedy. Some sections wanted to secede or to obtain greater autonomy. Taxation increased, graft and corruption spread, and there was a general breakdown of law and order.

The 1958 Revolution. Continued unrest and cultural differences between West and East Pakistan brought about a revolution in 1958. Martial law (government by the army) was declared and, in a coup, Field Marshal Muhammad Ayub Khan replaced Mirza as president. In an election in 1960 Ayub Khan was confirmed as president, and in 1965 he was reelected to a five-year term.

Under Ayub Khan's first administration, Pakistan enjoyed a relatively stable government and made progress culturally, economically, and politically. Martial law was ended in 1962 with the drafting of a new constitution providing for a stronger presidency.

When he took office in 1958, President Ayub Khan said, "Our ultimate aim is to restore democracy, but of the kind that people can understand and make work." He introduced what he called "Basic Democracies." This is a system of local self-government that begins at the village level. Each of the "Basic Democracies" represents a population unit of 1,000 people. Several villages are grouped together into a union council; these councils are then joined into sub-district councils, which are joined into district councils. At the top are division councils.

Each of the 12,000 basic units has ten elected members. These 120,000 members make up the Electoral College of Pakistan. They elect the president, the members of the National Assembly, and the provincial legislatures.

The local union councils are in charge of agricultural, industrial, and community development. They plan and construct roads, wells, irrigation canals, schools, and clinics. The money for these programs comes from taxes, tolls, and fees that the union council levies, in addition to contributions from the central government.

Under the New Constitution. A new constitution went into effect in 1962, providing for a president, a central legislature called the National Assembly, and a legislature with a governor in each province. The term of the president and the legislature is five years, and all are elected by the "Basic Democracies."

During his presidency, Ayub Khan established order in the country and drew up a program for Pakistan's economic growth. Refugees were moved out of cities and resettled in the countryside. The educational system was expanded. Land reform was adopted. Agricultural production and industrial growth were stimulated.

Revolt in East Pakistan. One of the major problems Ayub Khan had to face was the strong movement for greater autonomy in East Pakistan. Not long after he was reelected in 1965 for a second term as president, the internal problems between East and West Pakistan began to increase and came to the surface in many ways. The East Pakistanis felt they should have greater representation in the National Assembly because of their larger population. They also felt they were not well protected,

175

because the greater bulk of the Pakistani army was concentrated in West Pakistan. These feelings, coupled with the insistence that English be the official language, resulted in severe riots during the late 1960s. Ayub Khan was forced to retire in 1971 and was replaced by Agha Muhammad Yahya Khan. Once again Pakistan was placed under martial law.

Troops, mainly West Pakistanis, were sent into East Pakistan to put down the uprisings. Because of the inability of the army to control the rebellious East Pakistanis under normal martial law, it began a systematic program of terrorism in early 1971. Tens of thousands of East Pakistanis were killed, including large numbers of intellectuals and professional people. The result was open revolt by East Pakistanis against the Pakistani government. India joined the conflict on the side of the East Pakistanis, or Bengalis, after millions of them had fled to India to escape the slaughter. The result was the defeat of Pakistani forces and the creation of the new nation of Bangladesh in what had been East Pakistan. The nation called Pakistan now consisted only of what had formerly been West Pakistan.

In Search of Stability. A new Pakistani constitution was adopted in 1973. It provided for a bicameral legislature: the National Assembly with 200 members, having political power; and the Senate with 45 members. Fazal Elahi Chaudhri became president and Zulfiqar Ali Bhutto prime minister. Bhutto's policies of enforced land distribution and nationalization of industry aroused wide opposition. The result was the formation by nine opposition groups of the Pakistan National Alliance for the elections of 1977. Bhutto's party won the election, but charges of corruption were levied. General Muhammad Zia-ul-Haq imposed martial law and subsequently was appointed head of a new civilian regime. Bhutto was arrested and later executed. General Zia became President in September 1978.

In 1984, General Zia, despite earlier promises of a free election, assumed rule for another five years. Zia and other army officers ruled the country until 1988, when Zia was killed in a plane crash. Free elections were held later that year. The Pakistan People's party (PPP) emerged as the leading party, and its leader, Benazir Bhutto, daughter of Zulfiqar Ali Bhutto, became prime minister. Bhutto was successful in her dealings with foreign leaders, and a bank that she established to encourage industrial growth was remarkably successful. However, her bank was accused of favoring her friends and political associates in making loans, and in 1990 Bhutto was dismissed on charges of corruption.

After new elections, the Islamic Democratic Alliance took control of parliament. Its leader, Nawaz Sharif, became prime minister. Like Bhutto, Sharif adopted economic policies that seemed to be successful in building Pakistan's industry. In the Persian Gulf War of 1990-1991, however, Pakistan's neutrality angered Saudi Arabia and other Arab states, so that Pakistan lost valuable foreign aid from these countries.

By 1992 Pakistan's democracy had survived for four years. Although the possibility remained that the army would once again replace a democratic government with its own rule, every additional year made it likelier that democracy would survive.

THE GEOGRAPHIC AND CULTURAL BACKGROUND OF PAKISTAN

Although part of the subcontinent of India, the many differences in culture, language, and religion set Pakistan apart from Bangladesh and India.

Geography and Climate. Pakistan is made up of the former British India provinces of Sind, Northwest Frontier, Baluchistan, and West Punjab. The capital is Islamabad, and the largest city is Karachi.

There are two contrasting regions in Pakistan. In the east is an area of flat plains. In the north and west are hills, plateaus, and high mountains, including the Himalayas and the Hindu Kush. Most of Pakistan is mountainous or on a high plateau. The tall peaks of the Himalayas to the west and north of the Indus River, and the barren stretches of the Thar Desert to the east, contrast with the cultivated plains in the valley of the river and its tributaries.

The great Indus River, some 1,700 miles in length, rises in Tibet and, together with its five major tributaries, waters half of the land area of Pakistan. However, less than a quarter of this land is under cultivation. The average rainfall is only 10 inches a year, not enough for the country's agricultural needs. Therefore, irrigation is necessary for farming. There are more than 75,000 miles of irrigation canals in Pakistan, and the government is building more.

The climate of Pakistan varies considerably. In the northern regions it is chilly from autumn to spring. The summer months are hot everywhere. Rainfall is concentrated in the period from July to September, when the monsoon from the Bay of Bengal, far to the east, arrives with some of its moisture left over. This period coincides with the flooding of

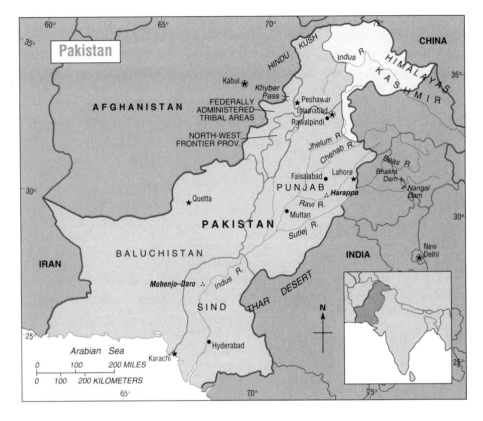

the Indus River, when the snows melt in the mountains. As a result, the water supply of Pakistan is adequate for only about three months of the year. That is why an extensive irrigation system had to be developed.

Peoples.   Pakistan was frequently invaded from the west through the passes in the Himalayas, especially the famous Khyber Pass in the Northwest Frontier Province. Its people are mainly of mixed Baluchi, Pathan, and Arab ancestry and differ markedly in customs, traditions, and languages, although Islam is a common element for the great majority (about 97 percent).

The Baluchi, said to be the descendants of Arabs who landed on the coast before the end of the 7th century, are nomads. The Pathans, related to the Afghanistani, consist of many tribes. Some of them are nomads who travel from pasture to pasture with their flocks of sheep and goats. Others are farmers who raise wheat and fruits. The Pathans are fierce fighters who frequently quarrel with each other over water rights or the scarce and valuable farm lands. Other peoples who live in

178

The Badshahi (royal) mosque in Lahore, Pakistan. The mosque was built in the Mogul era during the reign of Aurangzeb.

Pakistan include the Hunzas and Gilgitis, in the north; the Punjabis, in the eastern part of the territory; and the Sindhis, south of the Punjab.

Languages. Several languages are spoken in Pakistan. Most belong to the Indo-European family of languages. Some of these are Indo-Aryan languages, derived from Sanskrit, the ancient language of India. Others are Iranian languages, closely related to Farsi, the language of Iran. (See the map on page 15). In Karachi, Urdu is the principal spoken and written language. Urdu is similar to Hindi but with the addition of many Persian and Arabic words. It is written in the Arabic script. Urdu and English are the official languages and are taught in the schools. However, Pashto and Sindhi are spoken by about 15 percent of the people and Punjabi by even more. Brahui, Pakistan's only Dravidian language, is spoken by a small percentage of the people.

Pakistan, for many centuries the point of entry into the subcontinent of India, has been influenced by Arabic, Persian, Turkish, and European cultures. It was in the Indus River Valley at Mohenjo-Daro and Harappa that one of the earliest civilizations developed. The Aryans, who invaded this valley some 4,000 years ago and conquered the original inhabitants, left their mark on its present culture.

Agricultural and Industrial Products. About 75 percent of the approximately 113 million Pakistani inhabitants are engaged in agriculture. Among the principal crops are wheat, cotton, sugar, and tobacco. Wool and leather goods are important sources of income and valuable exports.

Pakistan's considerable mineral resources provide many jobs and are also important exports. Sizable deposits of limestone and gypsum provide materials for cement plants. Chromite is an exportable mineral, and graphite, rock salt, pottery clays, and glass sands are abundant. Half the country's fuel supply comes from the coal mined in Pakistan. Natural gas fields have been discovered in Baluchistan, and pipelines connect them to Karachi and Multan. Oil has been found, and intensive exploration promises further discoveries.

Land Reforms. More than half the land in Pakistan was farmed by tenant farmers. Some 6,000 large landowners controlled much of the land. The average farm owned by a farmer was less than four acres, too small to provide both food for his family and a cash income for necessities.

President Ayub Khan, after a report by a Land Reforms Commission for West Pakistan, adopted a program to redistribute the land. No person was allowed to own more than 500 acres of the 24 million acres of irrigated land, or 1,000 acres of unirrigated land. The state took over the surplus holdings and sold them to the farmers, preferably to the tenants on those same pieces of land. The old owners were compensated for the loss of their land; the new owners were expected to repay the cost of the purchase of the land over a 25-year period. Government-owned land was also divided and sold to the farmers. Money was lent to the new owners for the purchase of equipment. Other laws protected tenant farmers against high rent and from being forced off the land when they were working it. Over 2.5 million acres of land were redistributed, and some 75,000 landless farmers were settled on family farms.

Irrigation. Many projects have been completed in recent years or are nearing completion. Over 12 million additional acres of land have been brought under cultivation with the completion of these projects. The Food and Agriculture Organization of the United Nations continues to

In Pakistan, industrialization and urbanization proceed
at a rapid pace. Above, the industrial town of
Iskanderabad has a cement factory, a penicillin plant,
and a sugar factory. Below left, city officials discuss
plans for the development of Karachi, the industrial and
economic center of the country. However, in some areas
of Baluchistan, plows pulled by camels are still in use.

aid Pakistan in its efforts to extend the quantity and fertility of semi-arid farm land. However, subsistence farming remains the main occupation for most of the population.

Hydroelectric power is being generated from many irrigation projects. The projects provide power to operate the increasing number of factories in Pakistan and to electrify the villages. The Pakistan government plans to bring electricity to a thousand villages each year.

Industrial Growth. Foreign aid from the West has been a major factor behind Pakistan's remarkable industrial progress. The United States has contributed over $4 billion in economic and military assistance.

When independence came in 1947, there was little industry in Pakistan. Although Pakistan raised much of the subcontinent's raw materials, the great majority of the processing and milling plants were in India. Today, the state owns and controls over 7,000 miles of railroads, telecommunications, and part of the air transport industry. Most other industry is in private hands and operates on a capitalistic profit basis.

In the 1970s the government under President Ali Bhutto developed a series of measures designed to secure a more just and equitable distribution of national resources in order to ensure the flow of foreign investment and external aid. He established a board of industrial management to carry out industrial reforms. Labor reforms were also instituted with an increase of labor at the management level.

In the 1980s, Pakistan's economy plunged into crisis. A huge debt, dependence on foreign imports, and loss of U.S. aid contributed to the disaster. The rule of General Zia favored the great landlords and the rich. Since 1988, industrial development policies of Prime Ministers Benazir Bhutto and Nawaz Sharif have once again spurred Pakistan's industrial development.

FOREIGN RELATIONS

The creation of India and Pakistan in 1947 caused many problems that grew out of the division of the assets of the subcontinent. Ultimately, most of the problems were settled by negotiations. Some, such as the Kashmir boundary dispute (see pages 153–156), are still not resolved.

The India-Pakistan War of 1971 created new problems. The creation of the new nation of Bangladesh from what had been East Pakistan was long a source of friction between India and Pakistan.

Pakistan and Afghanistan.   The border between Pakistan and Afghanistan cuts through the tribes living in that area. The Pathans in Pakistan are related to the Afghans. For years after its independence, Pakistan was pressured by Afghanistan to allow the Pathans to join their own people on the other side of the frontier. When Pakistan refused to consider this, Afghanistan stopped trading with Pakistan. It also broke off diplomatic relations and turned to the Soviet Union for military equipment and the use of Soviet ports to ship Afghan goods. Through the efforts of the shah of Iran, acting as a mediator, the two countries resumed diplomatic relations in 1963.

In recent years, relations between the two countries have been strained, due to political instability in both nations. A civil war in Afghanistan, which began in 1980 and lasted ten years, caused a great

Afghani refugees from their country's civil war trek through a rugged mountain valley on their way to Pakistan.

crisis within Pakistan. More than 2.5 million Afghani refugees streamed into Pakistan, and a gigantic arms trade corrupted the Pakistani government. The aftermath of the war found thousands of Pakistanis involved in illegal trade in weapons and drugs.

Pakistan and China. When China invaded India in 1962, Pakistan noted that the bulk of India's armies remained near the Pakistan border and were not withdrawn to fight the invaders. The United States and Britain sent military supplies to the Indians, which angered the Pakistanis who claimed that this aid would be used against them and not the Chinese. In 1962, Pakistan signed a border treaty with China that ceded 13,000 square miles of Pakistani-held Kashmir to China. China agreed to support Pakistan's position on Kashmir and supported the Pakistanis in their wars with India in 1965 and 1971.

Relations with China improved throughout the 1970s and 1980s. The Chinese agreed to finance a major industrial complex. In the 1990s the Chinese were viewed as Pakistan's most important ally.

Pakistan and the United States. The relations between Pakistan and the United States have been cordial since 1947, although the United States halted all aid to both Pakistan and India after their 1965 war. Each country has resented the aid given by the United States to the other. India, particularly, has cooled off in its relations because of the position the United States took in the 1971 war. To India, this placed the United States and China in the position of defending Pakistani aggression against India, aiding the Bengali struggle for freedom.

In 1975 the U.S. government lifted a ten-year embargo on the export of arms to Pakistan. This led to closer ties, which had been developing since U.S. support of Pakistan in the Bangladesh civil war. From 1980 to 1990, the United States used Pakistan as a conduit for arms and supplies to Afghanistan. The two governments have had major disagreements over Pakistan's attempt to become a nuclear power.

Pakistan and the Future. As a new nation just accepted into the United Nations in 1947, the newly created state of Pakistan faced a bleak future. However, under the leadership and policies of Ali Jinnah, and later Ayub Khan, Pakistan became a respected member of the family of nations. Eventually, the budget was balanced and Pakistan exports and imports figured heavily in the world balance of trade.

Unfortunately, internal disputes with the eastern section of the country, so widely separated by India from the mainstream of government and the center of economic life, eventually resulted in civil war of ghastly proportions in 1971. When India entered the dispute, Pakistan was soundly defeated, and East Pakistan became the new nation of Bangladesh. For a time in 1972 it seemed that the entire economic and political structure of Pakistan might collapse.

President Zulfiqar Ali Bhutto, educated in the United States and England, imposed strict measures on the economy and the military. He reestablished relations with India and Bangladesh, and in 1973 war prisoners were exchanged. His successor, Muhammad Zia-ul-Haq, proclaimed Pakistan an Islamic republic in 1978 and promoted economic policies that favored rich landlords.

From 1980 to 1990 Pakistan's economy was disrupted by the flow of arms and other supplies to Afghanistan. The situation was aggravated by the Persian Gulf War of 1990–1991, which forced thousands of Pakistani workers to leave their well-paying jobs in Kuwait and Iraq. The money that these workers sent home had made an important contribution to Pakistan's economy. The collapse of the Soviet Union in 1991 left it uncertain what Pakistan's future role in its region might be.

BACKGROUND TO BANGLADESH INDEPENDENCE

Bangladesh, a nation created in 1971, was born out of bloodshed and brutal war. When Pakistan was created in 1947, it consisted of two widely separated sections. About the only common ground between the eastern and western sections was Islam. There was little else to hold the people together, for they differed in every other respect. Their land was different, their languages were different, and their pre-independence history was different.

One of the major problems that faced Pakistan throughout the nearly 25 years of its existence as East and West Pakistan was how to govern such a geographically widely separated nation. With the main seat of government in West Pakistan and the majority of its citizens living in East Pakistan, quarrels over representation and government reform arose almost from the beginning. In the east, the Awami League, composed of Bengalis of East Pakistan who were interested in greater autonomy for their section, was founded by Sheik Mujibur Rahman (usually referred to as Sheik Mujib).

In 1970, when East and West Pakistanis went to the polls to elect a new National Assembly, Awami League candidates received a clear majority—167 seats out of 313. The military government, under Ayub

Carrying their belongings, East Pakistanis flee toward the Indian border in order to escape the fighting between Bangladesh troops and regular Pakistani forces.

Khan, postponed convening the National Assembly. In March 1971, riots against the government broke out throughout East Pakistan. To make matters worse, East Pakistan in late 1970 had been subjected to one of the greatest natural disasters of all time. A cyclone and tidal wave had hit the land, killing an estimated 600,000 people. The Bengalis felt that the central government was indifferent to their tragedy and was not supplying sufficient aid.

Martial law was again imposed, and the army, largely West Pakistani, was sent to the East to put down the riots. What followed for the next nine months was probably one of the greatest bloodbaths in modern history as the army began a systematic slaughter of the Bengalis. Professional people and intellectuals especially were massacred. An estimated one million Bengalis were brutally killed in the ensuing conflict. Nearly 10 million people crossed the border to India to escape. Another 10 million were displaced within East Pakistan.

Finally India, which had officially recognized the independent state of Bangladesh on December 6, entered the conflict. In the two weeks that followed, Indian and Bengali forces defeated the Pakistani troops. The losses in terms of people and of damage to farmlands and industry were tremendous, but the Bengalis were determined to rebuild their country and faced the future with new hope and dedication. However, democracy never took root in Bangladesh, and a series of military juntas have been largely unsuccessful in coping with Bangladesh's many problems.

GEOGRAPHIC AND CULTURAL BACKGROUND OF BANGLADESH

Geography and Climate. Most of Bangladesh is fertile land and river delta. Climate ranges from cool dry winters to tropical wet summers. The average rainfall is over 100 inches a year, so there is no extensive need for irrigation projects as in Pakistan. Flood damage can be great during the monsoon season, as it was 1988 and 1989. Less frequent, but more devastating, are tropical storms. In 1991 a tropical storm struck Bangladesh's coastal areas, killing more than 50,000 people and millions of cattle and severely damaging the port city of Chittagong.

The major agricultural products are jute, rice, and tea. Some of the largest jute mills in the world are located in Bangladesh.

Peoples. The people of Bangladesh are said to be the descendants of the Dravidians, the earliest inhabitants of India, who were conquered by the Aryans. A large portion of the Bengali people were converted to Islam during the years of Mogul rule of India. The nation was continuously subordinated to other areas. In the late 19th century, the British began favoring Muslims for educational and governmental positions because of the growing Hindu-oriented nationalism.

Under British rule, Bengal was divided into eastern and western parts. East Bengal is the area that later became Bangladesh. West Bengal, with its capital at Calcutta and its largely Hindu population, remains part of India. After 1947, when East Bengal became East Pakistan, the area was largely controlled by the government of West Pakistan. Many Bengalis came to resent their lack of power. East Pakistan provided nearly two-thirds of Pakistan's exports and trade revenues, yet the needs of the people were often ignored. After unsuccessful protests by Bengali leaders in 1968 and 1969, civil war broke out in 1970. The war took a tremendous toll on the people of Bangladesh, and recovery has been a slow and painful process.

Social Life. At the end of the civil war, non-Bengali governmental and economic leaders left Bangladesh to return to West Pakistan. Opportunities became available for advancing into the empty positions, including high government offices and leadership of major industries. During the 1970s, Bengalis rose to positions of influence and power in the cities and countryside.

The role of women is still restricted. In the rural areas in particular, women rise in status and respect in their husbands' household as they

Bangladesh's largest export and the mainstay of the economy is jute. At top left, freshly harvested jute is prepared for its journey to Dhaka, where, top right, it is made into cloth at one of the world's largest textile mills. Below, workers prepare jute bales for export.

give birth to sons. Purdah (the seclusion of women) can be found in many villages. Segregation of the sexes even exists in social groups that have accepted modern Western cultural practices.

Cultural Life. The Bengalis are proud of their cultural heritage, including their language, forms of artistic expression, and religious background. The people have a reputation for being musical and poetic. Their strong national identity and sense of pride was a determining factor in the struggle to achieve independence.

The art and music of the Bengali people illustrates their close relationship with the land. The influence of Hinduism, Buddhism, and Islam is also apparent. The architecture in the cities shows the British influence. The government's support of education and the arts is indicative of the national commitment to the culture of the people.

The performing arts—dance, theater, and music—are firmly rooted in the history of the people. The impact of radio and television has spread rapidly in the past few years. Movies are also a popular form of entertainment.

Two weavers at work on a bamboo-and-wood loom in a Bangladesh village. The kind of cloth that they are weaving is one of the finest made on the Indian subcontinent.

189

THE GOVERNMENT OF BANGLADESH

Sheik Mujibur Rahman. Sheik Mujibur Rahman (Mujib) was the moving force in the Bengali independence movement. Shortly after the West Pakistanis invaded East Pakistan in March 1971, Mujib was captured and imprisoned. He was held in solitary confinement for nine months and, after Pakistan's defeat, was released by President Bhutto. Mujib returned to his country to find it in shambles.

Bangladesh began its existence with not much more than $500,000 in foreign exchange. The problems of rebuilding the torn nation were staggering. Putting a new government together was the top priority. Mujib, who had been named president while still in prison, adopted a provisional constitution for the state in 1972, naming a new cabinet with himself as prime minister. He arranged a 25-year treaty of friendship and a trade treaty with India. The United Nations and India provided food aid. Bangladesh was quickly recognized by most nations.

The Constitution of 1972 was approved by the Constituent Assembly in November of that year. It provided for a single-chamber parliament with 300 members elected by direct, universal adult suffrage and an additional 15 women to be elected by the 300 members. In March 1973, Sheik Mujib's party won an overwhelming election victory.

Reconstruction. The nation's reconstruction effort went forward slowly but steadily, until the worst floods in two decades crippled the nation during the summer of 1974. Bangladesh had to seek aid from other nations. The food supply was not sufficient for the nation's needs until 1976. Industrialization continued to increase, although at a rate below the stated goals. The economy was still sluggish.

The government continued to suffer from an inability to maintain law and order. A state of emergency was declared in December 1974. Political parties were banned and a presidential government installed. Under this government, the president took over most of the power in the country, at the expense of the elected parliament. Sheik Mujib became president and served until he was overthrown and killed in August 1975. His replacement as president lasted only three months, and the one after that lasted a year.

After Mujib's downfall, Pakistan was the first nation to recognize the new government, and formal diplomatic relations between Bangladesh and Pakistan were then established. The economy began to improve. The government permitted indoor meetings of political parties, beginning in late July 1976.

190

CASE STUDY:
United States Aid to Bangladesh

The following speech was made by Representative Herman Badillo (bah-DEE-yoh) of New York in the U.S. House of Representatives early in 1972:

> Mr. Speaker, during the brief but bitter fighting between India and Pakistan last month, the world bore witness to the folly of the ill-conceived policy of the United States toward India and, particularly, toward the struggle for independence in East Pakistan. For months prior to armed hostilities, the United States stood mute and failed to raise its voice against the reign of terror perpetrated against the Bengalis of East Pakistan by Punjabis from the West. While it is true that this was an internal struggle, this country or any other member of the family of free nations simply cannot ignore or condone the blatant violation of basic human rights and dignity which occurred in Bengal or the snuffing out of lives of men, women, and children at the whim of some brutal dictator. The acts of genocide committed in East Pakistan demanded that a hue and cry of protest be raised, yet this nation remained silent. . . .
>
> Mr. Speaker, time is long past due that the United States reassess its policy, both toward India and Bangladesh, and candidly admit its mistakes. By pursuing our present attitudes toward these two nations we have lost the faith of freedom-loving people throughout the world and are ignoring some of the basic principles upon which our own country was founded. . . .
>
> We must, therefore, enact legislation providing for immediate emergency aid to Bangladesh to help it overcome the devastation wrought by the war and to assist this new nation in effectively coping with its many economic and social problems.

Congressional Record. January 27, 1972.

1. From Congressman Badillo's speech, what do you infer was the policy of the United States toward Bangladesh at the time of its war for independence? Do you agree or disagree with Badillo's analysis and recommendation? Explain.
2. If you had been a member of Congress at that time, would you have advocated U.S. intervention in the Bangladesh situation? Explain.

The Zia Regime. In November 1976, Major General Ziaur Rahman (Zia) became chief martial law administrator. In a referendum in May 1977, an overwhelming majority confirmed Zia as president and approved his 19-point program committing the nation to Islam, restoring democracy, and promising economic and social progress and justice for the nation.

General Zia began a rural development program in order to gain support for his economic policies. The self-help scheme was based on reducing the number of unemployed people, which was estimated at between 6.9 and 9.7 million. His reconstruction program helped foster economic growth. He also continued the political reform program, removing the bans on political activities and holding a presidential election in June 1978 in which he was overwhelmingly reelected. He continued to relax martial law by reducing press censorship, releasing political prisoners, and permitting public meetings.

In 1981, Zia was assassinated. Through most of the 1980s, the government was headed by an army general, Hossein Muhammad Ershad. Ershad took most power into his own hands, restricting political parties and severely limiting civil rights. Pressure gradually built up for a return to democracy until, in 1990, Ershad, in turn, was deposed and arrested. Elections in 1991 led to a parliamentary government controlled by the Bangladesh National party with Begum Khalida Zia, widow of President Ziaur Rahman, as prime minister.

Bangladesh and the Future. Bangladesh faces an uncertain future. Its government has been unstable through most of its history. It is a terribly crowded country, the most densely populated in the world. From time to time it is struck by a terrible natural disaster, as in the tropical storms of 1970 and 1991.

Bangladesh seems likely to need foreign aid for many years to come. In Dhaka, the capital city of over four million people, Indians and Americans are much in evidence, as were Soviets at one time. Most are members of aid delegations, there to administer aid from their countries. U.S. aid has been substantial, more than Soviet aid but not as much as India has provided.

Bangladesh was admitted to the United Nations in 1974. It has been accepted into the British Commonwealth of Nations, which opens many doors in international trade and banking.

Chapter 8:
CHECKUP

REVIEWING THE CHAPTER

I. Building Your Vocabulary

In your notebook, write the correct term that matches the definition.

Urdu	Bengali	jute
martial law	East Pakistan	Awami League

1. plant fiber used primarily for sacking and twine
2. law applied by military, usually in occupied territory or during an emergency
3. political party that sought greater autonomy for East Pakistan
4. a person from East Pakistan, or Bangladesh
5. principal language of Karachi; a mixture of old Persian and Hindi with the addition of Turkish and Arabic words
6. the part of Pakistan that became Bangladesh

II. Understanding the Facts

In your notebook, write the numbers from 1 to 5. Write the letter of the correct answer to each question next to its number.

1. Before 1971, which major Asian country was divided into two parts 1,000 miles apart?
a. India b. Nepal c. Pakistan

2. Most of the people in Pakistan belong to which group?
a. Muslims b. Hindus c. Sikhs

3. The monsoons bring an abundance of rain to which country?
a. Pakistan b. Bangladesh c. Afghanistan

4. At the time of partition, where were most of the subcontinent's manufacturing plants?
a. Bangladesh b. Pakistan c. India

5. The governments of both Pakistan and Bangladesh have been troubled by:

a. frequent coups.

b. many splinter political parties.

c. lack of recognition by other nations.

III. Thinking It Through

In your notebook, write the numbers from 1 to 6. Write the letter of the correct conclusion to each sentence next to its number.

1. The major factor determining how India and Pakistan were divided was:

a. natural resources.	b. numbers of people.
c. religion.	d. language.

2. The Muslim League refused to support the Indian Congress Party because:

a. it wanted majority control in a united India.

b. it did not want to separate from Britain at that time.

c. it feared reprisals from the Bengalis of East Pakistan.

d. it favored a separate state for Muslims.

3. The Awami League of East Pakistan opposed the government in West Pakistan because:

a. the league wanted more representation for East Pakistan.

b. the league wanted to unite East Pakistan with India.

c. the league championed women's rights in Pakistan.

d. the league opposed military rule in Pakistan.

4. The person most responsible for the creation of Pakistan was:

a. Liaquat Ali Khan	b. Muhammad Ayub Khan.
c. Khandakar Mustaque Ahmed.	d. Muhammad Ali Jinnah.

5. Each of the following is a characteristic of Pakistan *except*:

a. need for irrigation.	b. industrial progress.
c. abundant rainfall.	d. mostly urban population.

6. Which of the following events did *not* occur in Bangladesh in the 1970s?

a. a cyclone, tidal waves, and monsoon floods.

b. systematic slaughter of Bengalis by the Pakistani military.

c. war with Indian and Bengali forces fighting Pakistani troops.

d. invasion by troops from China.

DEVELOPING CRITICAL THINKING SKILLS

1. In what way are the reasons for the birth of Pakistan similar to the reasons for the birth of Bangladesh?
2. Suggest reasons to explain the instability of governments in both Pakistan and Bangladesh.
3. Were there ways that Britain could have prevented the tragic massacres that accompanied the partition of India? Explain.
4. Why did India join the Bengalis in their fight against Pakistan?
5. The world market for jute was in decline in the early 1990s. Explain what effects that decline might have on Bangladesh.

INTERPRETING A CHART

The chart on page 196 compares Bangladesh and Pakistan in a number of different ways. Use the chart to answer the following questions. Write the answers in your notebook.

1. How many more people total are there in Bangladesh than in Pakistan? How many more people are there per square mile?
2. Which industries, crops, and minerals do the two nations have in common?
3. Which nation has the most arable land? Which nation has the highest GNP?
4. In which nation would you be more likely to own a radio, television, or telephone?
5. What do you learn about a nation when you know how many motor vehicles it operates?
6. Write one generalization based on the information in the chart.

INTERPRETING A MAP

Study the map of Pakistan on page 178 and answer the questions that follow. Write the answers in your notebook.

Comparison of Pakistan and Bangladesh

	BANGLADESH	PAKISTAN
Population	117,976,000 (1990)	113,163,000
Population Density	2,028 per square mile	335 per square mile
Urban	22% (1988)	32%
Government	presidential/parliamentary	parliamentary democracy
Industries	cement, jute, textiles, fertilizers, petroleum products	textiles, fool processing, chemicals, tobacco
Crops	jute, rice, tea	rice, wheat
Minerals	natural gas, offshore oil	natural gas, iron ore
Arable Land	67%	26%
GNP	$20.2 billion (1989)	$40 billion
Imports	$3.6 billion (1989)	$7.3 billion (1990)
Exports	$1.3 billion (1989)	$5.5 billion (1990)
Motor Vehicles	39,000 passenger cars 51,000 commercial vehicles	540,000 passenger cars 158,000 commercial vehicles
Radios	1 per 24 persons	1 per 11 persons
Television Sets	1 per 315 persons	1 per 73 persons
Telephones	1 per 572 persons	1 per 159 persons
Hospital Beds	1 per 3,233 persons	1 per 1,783 persons
Physicians	1 per 6,166 persons	1 per 2,081 persons
Literacy	29%	26%

196

1. What nations share borders with Pakistan?
2. Why has the Khyber Pass been important to the area of present-day Pakistan throughout its history?
3. What is the capital of Pakistan?
4. In what general direction is Kashmir from Karachi?

ENRICHMENT AND EXPLORATION

1. Find out about the role played by Pakistan and Bangladesh in the Persian Gulf War of 1991. Present your findings in a short report to the class. Why are Pakistan and Bangladesh concerned about events in the Middle East?

2. Find out what jute looks like and how it is grown and processed. In what ways is jute a good product for a nation such as Bangladesh?

3. Read a book about everyday life in Pakistan. Report to the class on the farming work at various times of the year, about the Islamic calendar and feast days, about the ceremonies for important events such as marriages, births, and funerals.

4. Prepare a report describing Islamabad, the capital of Pakistan, and Lahore, one of its great cities, for potential tourists. Use current travel guides from the local library to help you.

Glossary

alluvium (uh-LOO-vee-uhm): topsoil washed down by rivers from higher elevations and deposited on lower ground

Amritsar Massacre (uhm-RIT-suhr): a violent attack by British troops on a protest meeting in the Punjab in 1919

Aryan (AIR-ee-uhn): one of a Caucasian people who migrated to the Indus River Valley around 2500 B.C.

Awami League (ah-WAH-mee): political party that sought greater autonomy for East Pakistan

Basic Democracies: system of local self-government in Pakistan that begins at the village and reaches to the national government

Basic Education: the teaching of home skills and crafts in addition to basic skills

bazaar: a market or street of open shops

Bengali (ben-GAH-lee): a person from Bengal; also, the language of Bengal

Brahman (BRAH-muhn): the Supreme Being in the Hindu belief; also, the highest, or priestly, caste

British East India Company: private trading company that had a monopoly on British trade with India, China, and the East Indies

Buddhism (BOO-diz-uhm): religion that developed in India in the 6th and 5th centuries B.C.; although very important in other Asian countries, it has almost disappeared in India

caste: one of the hereditary classes that divide Hindu society

cease-fire agreement: truce

centralized: controlled by one central government

civil disobedience: refusal to obey laws regarded as unjust as a method of forcing reform

civil service: the nonmilitary employees of a government

Community Development: a national educational program designed to raise agricultural production with the voluntary cooperation of the farmers

Congress Party: the first Indian political party, leader in the fight for independence and, since 1947, the predominant party in Indian politics

cooperative: an agricultural association in which farmers combine small holdings into large farms that they work together

cottage industry: an industry whose goods are produced by people working at home

cremation (kree-MAY-shuhn): the burning of a corpse

Dalai Lama (dahl-EYE LAH-muh): religious and political leader of the Tibetans

deity: a god or goddess

delta: a low-lying area at the mouth of a river formed by deposits of silt from the river

dharma (DUHR-muh): set of rules that Hindus believe each living thing must follow to be promoted in its next reincarnation

domesticate: to tame (animals) and breed them for human use

Dravidian (druh-VID-ee-uhn): one of earliest inhabitants of the Indus River

Valley; also, a family of languages spoken by these peoples and now predominant in the southern part of India

East Pakistan: the part of Pakistan that became Bangladesh

Empress of India: title assumed by Queen Victoria

enclave (EHN-klayv): a country or part of a country lying wholly within the boundaries of another nation

Five Year Plan: a highly planned economic program directed by the government

Government of India Act of 1935: British law that gave complete autonomy to the provinces and created a federal system to govern India upon independence

gram sevak: under the Community Development program, a government officer in charge of a block of villages

Green Revolution: increase in India's output of wheat and rice, due to the use of new types of grains, more fertilizer, and improved irrigation

Gupta (GOOP-tah): dynasty that ruled northern India beginning in the 4th century A.D.

Gurkha (GOOR-kah): a member of the warrior class of Nepal

Hindi (HIN-dee): one of India's two official languages

Hinduism (HIN-doo-iz-uhm): the largest religion in India; it is also a social system and a philosophy

Indo-Aryan: a family of languages derived from Sanskrit and spoken in much of the Indian subcontinent

Indo-Iranian: a family of languages spoken in Iran and in neighboring regions of Pakistan

Indus River Agreement: agreement that resolved conflict between Pakistan and India about the use of the rivers that flow through both countries

Iron Pillar: monument erected near Delhi to commemorate one of Chandragupta's victories

Islam (IS-lahm): the second largest religion of the Indian subcontinent; its followers, called Muslims, worship one God, Allah

Jainism (JEYEN-iz-uhm): a religion of India whose adherents practice nonviolence to all living things

jajmani: payment for services with food

jute (JOOT): a plant fiber used primarily for sacking and twine

karma (KAHR-muh): Hindu belief that people's actions in life determine their future states

Kashmir (KASH-mihr): Indian state; control of Kashmir is disputed by Pakistan and India

Kashmir plebiscite: promised, but never-held, vote in Kashmir to determine whether that state would join India or Pakistan

Kshatriya: the warrior caste and ruling aristocracy

land reform: distribution by the government of land among the people

Mahabharata (muh-HUH-BAH-ruh-tuh): epic that contains the *Bhagavad-Gita,* the story of Arjuna, the perfect warrior

Maratha (muh-RAH-tuh): one of a people of the Western Ghat mountains who resisted the Moguls and established a strong state in central and western India

martial law: law applied by the military, usually in occupied territory or during an emergency

Maurya (MAH-oor-yah): Indian empire founded in northeastern India by Chandragupta Maurya in 332 B.C.

Mogul (MOH-guhl): a descendant of Mongol invaders of India who ruled a great empire in India from 1525 until 1858

monopoly: exclusive ownership or control

monsoon (mahn-SOON): a wind that brings the rainy season when it blows from the ocean

Montagu-Chelmsford Reforms: reforms adopted in 1919 that gave some power to provincial legislatures and to a federal legislative assembly, but reserved much power for the viceroy

Morley-Minto Reforms: reforms of 1909 that permitted Muslims to have separate representation in the legislature

Muslim: a follower of Islam

Muslim League: political party founded in 1906 to compete with the Hindu-dominated Congress Party

neutralism: policy of not taking sides in international disputes

nonalignment: policy of not participating in political or military blocs, but deciding each question of foreign policy individually

panchayat (PAHN-chah-yaht): village council

Panch Shila (PAHNCH SHEE-lah): 1954 agreement between India and China, stating the principles of their relationship

Parsi (PAHR-see): a Zoroastrian descended from refugees who fled from Persia in the 7th and 8th centuries

Pathan (puh-TAHN): one of a nomadic people of Pakistan related to the people of Afghanistan

Pondichéry (pong-dee-shay-REE): location of trading post of the French East India Company

raga (RAH-guh): a form of Indian music

Rajput (RAHJ-poot): kings of northwestern India from the 8th to the 13th centuries who tried to stop the Muslim advance.

Ramayana (rah-MAH-yuh-nuh): Hindu epic that tells the story of the god Rama and his wife Sita

reincarnation (ree-in-kahr-NAY-shun): Hindu belief that upon death, a person's soul moves into the body of another living thing

Rig-Veda (rig-VAY-duh): the oldest religious document in history; it contains a "Hymn of Creation"

Salt March: Gandhi's dramatic walk to the sea in protest of a British tax on salt

Sanskrit (SAN-skrit): ancient language of India that is related to many other languages of Europe and the Middle East

satyagraha (SUHT-yuh-gruh-huh): Gandhi's concept of "soul force," the power of goodness

Scheduled Castes: legal name for those formerly called "Untouchable," reflecting the fact that a certain percentage of government jobs are reserved for these people

sepoy: an Indian serving in the army of a European power

Sepoy Mutiny: another term for the Great Indian Mutiny of 1857

shellac: a wood finish made from substances deposited on trees by insects

Shudra: the servant caste

Sikh (SEEK): a follower of a religion that combines elements of Hinduism and Islam

standard of living: the way of life, including necessities and luxuries, to which a person is accustomed

subcaste: a caste that is part of another, larger caste

subcontinent: a large landmass that is part of a larger continent but separated from it by natural barriers and by differences in culture

Taj Mahal (TAZH muh-HAHL): famous tomb built at Agra by the Mogul Shah Jahan for his wife; the greatest masterpiece of Indian architecture

tariff: a tax on imports or exports

Tashkent Accord (tash-KENT): agreement between India and Pakistan to halt fighting in 1966 and to return to positions held before conflict began in 1965

Tata Works: steel plants and other factories owned by one Indian family

thatch: roofing of straw, palm leaves, or similar material

turban: a long piece of cloth worn wrapped around the head

Untouchables: the persons at the lowest level of the caste system

Upanishads (oo-PAN-ih-shadz): commentaries on the individual soul and the origin of the universe

Urdu (OOR-doo): a main language of Pakistan; similar to Hindi, but with many words of Persian and Arabic origin, and written in the Arabic script

Vaisya: the farmer, professional, and artisan caste

viceroy: the head of the British government in India

zamindar (zuh-meen-DAHR): a former tax collector who became a landlord under British rule

Bibliography

Chapter 1

Archer, Mildred. *Early Views of India*. London: Thames & Hudson, 1980.

Time-Life Books. *India*. Alexandria, VA: Time-Life Books, 1987.

Frater, Alexander. *Chasing the Monsoon*. New York: Alfred A. Knopf, 1991.

Huyler, Stephen P. *Village India*. New York: Harry N. Abrams, 1985.

Lewis, Norman. *A Goddess in the Stones: Travels in India*. London: Jonathan Cape, 1991.

Singh, Madanjiet. *This My People*. New York: Rizzoli International Publications, 1989.

Theroux, Paul, and Steve McCury. *The Imperial Way*. Boston: Houghton Mifflin, 1985.

Chapter 2

Beach, Milo Cleveland. *The Adventures of Rama*. illus. Washington, DC: Freer Gallery of Art, Smithsonian Institution, 1983.

Chopra, P.N. *Religions and Communities of India*. Atlantic Highlands, NJ: Humanities Press, 1982.

McLeod, W. Hew. *The Sikhs: History, Religion and Society*. New York: Columbia University Press, 1989.

Tillis, Malcolm, and Cynthia Giles. *Turning East: New Lives in India*. New York: Paragon House, 1989.

Wolpert, Stanley. *India*. Berkeley, CA: University of California Press, 1991.

Chapter 3

Broehl, Wayne G., Jr. *Crisis of the Raj*. Hanover, NH: University Press of New England, 1986.

Embree, Ainslie T. *Sources of Indian Tradition*. Vol. I: *From the Beginning to 1800*. 2nd ed. New York: Columbia University Press, 1988.

Nyrop, Richard F., ed. *India, a Country Study*. 4th ed. Foreign Area Studies, The American University. Washington, DC: Department of the Army, 1985.

Wolpert, Stanley. *A New History of India*. 3rd ed. New York: Oxford University Press, 1989.

Chapter 4

Fabb, John. *India: The British Empire from Photographs*. London: B.T. Batsford, 1986.

Fisher, Michael Herbert. *A Clash of Cultures: Adwadh, the British, and the Mughals.* Riverdale, MD: Riverdale, 1987.
Hay, Stephan. *Sources of Indian Tradition.* Vol. II: *Modern India and Pakistan.* 2nd ed. New York: Columbia University Press, 1988.
Moorhouse, Geoffrey. *India Britannica.* London: Harvill Press, 1983.
Trevelyan, Raleigh. *The Golden Oriole.* New York: Viking, 1987.

Chapter 5

Akbar, M.J. *India: The Siege Within.* New York: Viking Penguin, 1985.
Brass, Paul R. *The New Cambridge History of India. IV. 1: The Politics of India Since Independence.* New York: Cambridge University Press, 1990.
Brown, Judith M. *Gandhi: Prisoner of Hope.* New Haven: Yale University Press, 1989.
Collins, Larry, and Dominique LaPierre. *Freedom at Midnight.* London: Pan Books, 1977.
Embree, Ainslie T. *Imagining India: Essays on Indian History.* New York: Oxford University Press, 1989.
Fischer, Louis. *Life of Mahatma Gandhi.* New York: New American Library, 1950.
Tully, Mark, and Zareer Masani. *India: Forty Years of Independence.* New York: George Braziller, 1988.

Chapter 6

Borden, Carla M. *Contemporary Indian Tradition: Voices on Culture, Nature, and the Challenge of Change.* Washington, DC: Smithsonian Institution Press, 1989.
Fishlock, Trevor. *Gandhi's Children.* New York: Universe Books, 1983.
Massey, Reginald, ed. *All India: A Catalog of Everything Indian.* Secaucus, NJ: Chartwell Books, 1986.

Chapter 7

Akbar, M. J. *Nehru: The Making of India.* London: Viking Penguin, 1988.
Bradnock, Robert. *India's Foreign Policy Since 1971.* New York: Council on Foreign Relations Press, 1990.
Moraes, Dom. *Indira Gandhi.* Boston: Little, Brown, 1986.
Nehru, Jawaharlal. *Jawaharlal Nehru: An Autobiography.* New York: Oxford University Press, 1989.
Nehru, Jawaharlal. *Toward Freedom.* New York: John Day, 1941.

Chapter 8

Bhutto, Benazir. *Daughter of Destiny: An Autobiography.* New York: Simon & Schuster, 1989.

Burke, Shahid Javed. *Pakistan: A Nation in the Making.* New York: Oxford University Press, 1986.

Burke, Shahid Javed, and Craig Baxter. *Pakistan Under the Military: Eleven Years of Zia ul-Haq.* Boulder, CO: Westview Press, 1991.

Heitzman, James and M.R.L. Worden, eds. *Bangladesh: A Country Study.* Federal Research Division of the Library of Congress, Area Handbook Program. Washington, DC: U.S. Government Printing Office, 1989.

Khan, Imran. *Indus Journey: A Personal View of Pakistan.* London: Chatto & Windus, 1990.

Reeves, Richard. *Passage to Peshawar.* New York: Simon & Schuster, 1984.

Suleri, Sara. *Meatless Days.* Chicago: University of Chicago Press, 1987.

Index

industry in India, 127
British Commonwealth of Nations, 192
British Dominion Act (1935), 174
British East India Company, 75, 77, 78, 81, 133,
British India, 81
Buddha, 46-47 See also Siddhartha Gautama.
Buddhism, 45-47, 58, 63, 163, 189
Burma, 78, 99 See Myanmar.
Burning Ghats, 39
bustees (slum dwellings), 139

Calcutta, 18, 25, 75, 82, 139, 187
Calicut, 74
Cape Comorin, 1, 13
Cape of Good Hope, 74
Carter, President Jimmy, 161
caste system, 33, 40-43, 48, 58, 79, 171
  in Bengal, 65
  and individual liberties, 106
  in Nepal and Bhutan, 163
  under British rule, 143
cattle, sacred, 39, 41, 58, 79
Cauvery river, 12
Ceylon, See Sri Lanka.
Chanderagnor, 152
Chandigarh, 141
Chandragupta I and II, 62, 63
chappati, 14, 17
charpoy, 16-17
chatai, 17
Chenab, 153
Cherrapunji, 10
China,
  Buddhism in, 46
  India and, 158-159
  language of, 13
  Nepal and, 163
  political influence of, 129
  Tibetan revolt against, 158
  trade with, 63, 120
  war with India, 120, 154, 158
Chittagong, 19, 187
Christianity, 45, 49, 79
civil service examinations, 93-94
climate, subcontinental, 7-11
Clive, Robert, 75, 76, 77
Community Development Programs, 120, 121-123, 135
Congress Party, 99, 107, 129
  defeat of, 111
  formation of, 93-94
  Jinna and, 172
  Nehru and, 109
  reorganization of, 108
  Shastri and, 110

Congress (I) Party, 108, 112
Constantinople, 73-74
Constituent Assembly, 172, 190
constitution, Bangladesh, 190
constitution, India, 41, 98
  amended, 105
  individual liberties under, 106-107, 131, 144
  cooperatives, 125
Cornwallis, Lord, 77-78
cottage industry, 27, 129, 139
cotton, 21, 26, 56, 74, 86
"Council of States", 105
cremation, 11, 39
Curzon, Lord, 94

Dalai Lama, 158
Dalhousie, Lord, 78
Damão, 74, 153
Damascus, 65
dance, 141-142
Darius I, 58
Dasratha, King, 37
Deccan plateau, 2, 6, 8, 10, 12, 13, 18, 21, 59, 61
deities, 34
Delhi, 18, 25, 44, 66, 68, 79, 141
Delhi, Sultanate of, 65
Department of Public Instruction, 78
Desai, Morarji, 108, 111
Devi, 34, 58
Dhaka, 19, 25, 155, 188
dharma, 38, 40, 43, 58
Discovery of India, The, Nehru, 109
Diu, 74, 152
domestication of animals, 57
Dravidian language, 13, 179
Dravidian peoples, 40, 57, 62, 187
Dupleix, Joseph, 75
Durgapur, 128
dyarchy, 95

East India Company, British, 75, 77, 78, 81, 133
East India Company, French, 75
East Indies, 62, 73, 74, 75
East Pakistan,
  and creation of Bangladesh, 182, 185
  revolt (1965), 175-176
  revolution (1958), 174
education, 78, 131-136
Egypt, 65
Eightfold Path, 47
Elahi Chaudhri, Fazal, 176
Electoral College of Pakistan, 175
English language, 13, 15, 16, 93, 133, 135, 137

Ershad, Hossein Muhammad, 192

Fa-Hsien, 62
Farsi language, 15, 179
film, 142, 143
"First War of Indian Independence",
 79-80
Five Pillars of Islam, 43
Five Year Plans, 109, 119-120, 127,
 139, 156
food, 17, 20
Ford Foundation, 130
forests, 24-25
Four Noble Truths, 47
Fourteen Points, 95
France, 65, 152
French and Indian War, 75
French East India Company, 75

Gama, Vasco da, 74
Gandhi, Indira, 41, 107, 110, 111,
 121, 144, 162
 illegal election practices of,
  108
 and peace with Pakistan, 155
 violations of human rights
  under, 160
 visits Moscow, 157
Gandhi, Mohandas (Mahatma), 37,
 121, 143, 151, 173
 death of 101-102
 early life of, 96
 education program of, 135
 and noncooperation, 97-98
 and Untouchables, 40-41
Gandhi, Rajiv, 108, 112, 159, 161,
 162
Ganga Mata, 12
Ganges Canal, 78
Ganges River, 5, 6, 8, 10, 11-12,
 20, 26, 39
Ganges River valley, 58
Gautama, Siddhartha, 46, 58 See
 also Buddha.
Genghis Khan, 65-66
Germany, 99
Ghats, Eastern and Western, 2, 6,
 10, 20, 68
ghee, 17
Ghori, Muhammad, 65
Gilgiti peoples, 179
Glimpses of World History, Nehru,
 109
Goa, 74, 152, 156
Godavari river, 12
Godse, N.V., 101
Gokhale, Gopal K., 94
Golden Temple, 48
Government of India Act (1935), 98

gram sevak, 121-122
Granth Sahib, 48
Great Bengali Famine, 99
"Great Indian Mutiny", 79-80
Great Uprising of 1857, 79-80
Greece, 58
Greek invaders, 61
"Green Revolution", 21, 121
Gujarat, 96
Gupta dynasty, 62
Gurkhas, 162
guru, 47

hajj, 43
Hanuman, 37
Harappa, 56, 179
harijans, 40, 41, 42, 97
Harsha, King, 62
Hastings, Warren, 77, 78
Himalayas, 1, 2-3, 5, 7, 10, 11,
 20, 58, 164, 177, 178
Hindi language, 13, 15, 16, 80,
 135, 179
Hindu Kush mountains, 2, 3, 177
Hindu University, 137
Hinduism, 20, 33-34, 45, 57-58, 78,
 arts and, 141
 in Bangladesh, 189
 in Bhutan, 163
 birth control and, 126
 caste system and, 40-43
 chief religious ideas of, 38
 dietary laws of, 17, 22
 Gandhi and, 97
 Ganges and, 11-12
 Islamic period and, 64-65
 in Nepal, 163
 Pakistan and, 152, 172
 religious practices of, 39
 since independence, 144
 sources of, 34
 stories of, 35-37
"House of the People", 105
Hsüan-Tsang, 62
Hume, Allan O., 93
Huns, 64
Hunza peoples, 179
Hyderabad, 18, 77, 78, 81, 103
hydroelectric power, 25, 131, 132,
 182
"Hymn of Creation", 34
ibn Kasim, Muhammad, 65
Independence Day, 98, 101
Indian Civil Service, 77, 78, 82,
 84, 85
Indian Military Academy, 85
Indian National Congress, 93, 95,
 98, 101
Indian Ocean, 1, 5, 9

Photograph Acknowledgements: Page 3, UPI Bettman; 5, © Earl Kowall/Gamma Liaison; 12, © Robert Nickelsberg/Gamma Liaison; 14 (top, middle), Look Magazine; 14 (bottom), Unicef; 17, Look Magazine; 19, United Nations/J.P. Laffonte; 22, Reuters/Bettmann; 26, © Udi Herzog/FPG; 35, Bettmann; 36 (top), Metropolitan Museum of Art, Eggleston Fund, 1927; 36 (bottom), Mathura Museum; 39, © M. Bryan Ginsberg; 44, © Steve Vidler/Nawrocki Stock Photo; 46, Bettmann; 48, Reuters/Bettmann; 56, © Paolo Koch/Photo Researchers; 61, Art Resource; 63, AP/Wide World Photo; 67 (top), Metropolitan Museum of Art, Gift of Alexander Smith Cochran; 67 (bottom), India Goverment Tourist Office; 76, Culver Pictures; 80, Bettmann; 82, Konran Media, Inc.; 83, Bettmann; 89, Bettmann; 96, Culver Pictures; 100, UPI/Bettmann; 110 (top), Bettmann Archive; 110 (bottom), UPI/Bettmann; 111 (left), Wide World Photos; 111 (right), United Nations; 112, Gamma Liaison; 119, Look Magazine; 120, United Nations/Ray Witlin; 122 (top), New York Times; 122 (bottom), United Nations; 124, United Nations; 127, United Nations/T.S. Saytan; 128, © Steve Vidler/Nawrocki; 130, Gamma Liaison; 132, United Nations; 134, © M. Bryan Ginsberg; 137, © Mimi Forsyth/Monkmeyer Press; 138, United Nations/C. Srinivasan; 140, © Jean Kugler/FPG; 142 (top), Bartholomew/Gamma Liaison; 142 (bottom), Photofest; 154, Government of India Tourist Office; 155, UPI/Bettmann; 157, UPI/Bettmann; 162, UPI/Bettmann; 164 (top), © Alain Buu/Gamma Liaison; 164 (bottom), Reuters/Bettmann; 173, UPI/Bettmann; 179, United Nations; 181, United Nations; 183, UPI/Bettmann; 186, UPI/Bettmann; 188, United Nations; 189, Reuters/Bettmann.